S0-CJC-037

LINGUISTIC ANALYSIS
AND
TEXT INTERPRETATION

*Essays on the Bill of Rights and on
Keats, Shakespeare and Dreiser*

Juhani Rudanko

University Press of America, Inc.
Lanham • New York • Oxford

WINGATE UNIVERSITY LIBRARY

Copyright © 1997 by
University Press of America,® Inc.
4720 Boston Way
Lanham, Maryland 20706

12 Hid's Copse Rd.
Cummor Hill, Oxford OX2 9JJ

All rights reserved
Printed in the United States of America
British Library Cataloguing in Publication Information Available

Library of Congress Cataloging-in-Publication Data

Rudanko, Martti Juhani.
Linguistic analysis and text interpretation : essays on the Bill of Rights
and on Keats, Shakespeare, and Dreiser / Juhani Rudanko.
p.   cm.
Includes bibliographical references and index.
1. English language--Discourse analysis. 2. United States--
Constitutional law--Amendments--1st-10th. 3. Shakespeare, William,
1564-1616--Language 4. Dreiser, Theodore, 1871-1945--Language.
5. Keats, John, 1795-1821--Language. 6. Discourse analysis,
Literary. 7. Written communication. I. Title.
PE1422.R83   1997   420'.1'41--dc21   97-9489 CIP

ISBN 0-7618-0734-9 (cloth: alk. ppr.)
ISBN 0-7618-0735-7 (pbk: alk. ppr.)

⊖™ The paper used in this publication meets the minimum
requirements of American National Standard for information
Sciences—Permanence of Paper for Printed Library Materials,
ANSI Z39.48—1984

Acknowledgments

Substantial parts of two chapters of this book have been published in article form. Parts of chapter 3 appeared in *Multilingua* 14, no. 4 (1995), 391-409, under the title "The Bill of Rights in the Balance: the Debate of June 8, 1789" and parts of chapter 6 appeared in *Estudios Ingleses de la Universidad Complutense* 4 (1996), 11-22, under the title "Pleading with an Unreasonable King: on the Kent and Pauline Episodes in Shakespeare." Further, parts of chapter 5 are scheduled to appear in *Language and Style* in early 1997, prior to the publication of this book. I am indebted to Mouton de Gruyter, a Division of Walter de Gruyter & Co., for permission to reprint material that originally appeared in article form in *Multilingua*, to Professor Angela Downing, editor of *Estudios Ingleses de la Universidad Complutense,* for permission to reprint material that originally appeared in that periodical, and to Queen's College Press for permission to reprint material that is scheduled to appear first in *Language and Style.*

Further, I am indebted to the following publishers and copyright holders: Thomas Nelson and Sons Limited, UK, for permission to quote selected extracts out of the Arden Shakespeare Series 1) *Othello,* edited by M. Ridley, 2) *King Lear,* edited by K. Muir, 3) *The Winter's Tale,* edited by J. Pafford, and 4) *Coriolanus,* edited by P. Brockbank; Harvard University Press, for permission to reprint John Keats's poem *To Autumn* from *The Poems of John Keats,* edited by Jack Stillinger, copyright © 1978 by the President and Fellows of Harvard College. Reprinted by permission of Harvard University Press; W. W. Norton & Company, for permission to quote selected material from Theodore Dreiser's *Sister Carrie: A Norton Critical Edition,* edited by Donald Pizer; the Finnish publishing house Otava, for permission to quote selected material from *William Shakespearen Suuret Draamat II* [William Shakespeare's Great Plays II]. *Hamlet, Othello,* suomentanut [translated into Finnish by] Yrjö Jylhä, copyright © Otava, and Mr. Hanno Eskola, for permission to quote selected material from William Shakespeare, *Othello,* suomentanut [translated into Finnish by] Hanno Eskola.

I also want to express my thanks to the University of Tampere, the Department of English of the University of Tampere, and the Academy of Finland for promoting the completion of this book.

I owe a deep debt of gratitude to Ian Gurney, of the University of Tampere, for reading, and commenting on, the chapters of this book, including their early stages. I am also grateful to Robert MacGilleon, of the University of Tampere, for reading, and commenting on, the next to final version of this book. Further, I am indebted to Maija Viitanen, my assistant at the University of Tampere, for the care with which she checked the manuscript. She also provided indispensable help with the task of compiling the index. Beyond the people mentioned here, a number of others helped with some of the individual chapters, as is acknowledged in the appropriate chapters. For all the shortcomings that remain in the book, the responsibility rests squarely with me as the sole author.

Tampere   Juhani Rudanko

Contents

Chapter 1 Introduction   1

Chapter 2 The Bill of Rights and
           the Debate of June 8, 1789   5
               The Bill of Rights
               and its World-Wide Import   5
               The Context of the Debate   9
               The Sequence of Speeches   11

Chapter 3 Rhetoric of Reaction in the Debate
           of June 8, 1789   19
               Notes to Chapter 3   33

Chapter 4 Rhetorical Styles in the Debate
           of June 8, 1789   35
               Speeches by Opponents   36
               Madison's Rhetorical Style   45
               Conclusion   47
               Notes to Chapter 4   48
               Appendix   49
                   Texts of Key Speeches   49
                   What Happened Later   55

Chapter 5 Process and Activity in *To Autumn*   59
               Notes to Chapter 5   68

Chapter 6   Pleading with an Unreasonable King:
             the Kent and Pauline Episodes
             in Shakespeare   71
                 Notes to Chapter 6   85
                 Coda: Discretionary and Non-Discretionary
                 Acts and Actions in Shakespeare   86

Chapter 7   Case Roles in Literary Translation:
             an Example from Shakespeare   89
                 Notes to Chapter 7   101

Chapter 8   Interpreting *Othello* in a Popularizing
             Finnish Production   103

Chapter 9   Not Making a Choice in Dreiser: the Leadup
             to Hurstwood's Theft in *Sister Carrie*   111
                 Notes to Chapter 9   118

Chapter 10   Concluding Observations   119

             References   123

             Index   133

Chapter 1

Introduction

The present book has two chief objectives. One is to apply a range of analytical methods to the study of selected texts in order to shed fresh light on their interpretation. The other objective is of a methodological character: it is hoped that the application of these analytical methods, sometimes originally worked out in the abstract, to actual concrete texts may contribute to the further development and refinement of such methods.

The analytical methods to be applied in this book are all linguistic or rhetorical in nature. They vary in the different chapters, depending on the properties and peculiarities of the particular texts involved. Both documentary and literary texts are investigated. The documentary text examined is the record of an important debate in the United States House of Representatives. In the sphere of literature, the texts selected range from the genre of poetry to the genres of drama and the novel.

In the first part of the book, chapters 2, 3, and 4, the focus is on the United States Bill of Rights and especially on the debate of June 8, 1789 in the United States House of Representatives. It was in the course of this debate that James Madison introduced his proposals for amendments, which were to form the key elements of the United States Bill of Rights. However, the reaction in the House to his motion to introduce amendments was so hostile on that day that he may well have wondered if his propositions would ever get off the ground. If his propositions had been voted down or if the subject had been postponed till the following year, as was proposed in the course of the debate, it is impossible to say whether they would ever have been approved, for even a postponement till the following year might well have meant that the first Congress could not have finished the task of considering amendments and there is no way of saying what the second Congress might have done.

In the event, Madison's propositions were neither voted down nor was the subject postponed till the following year. Instead, the outcome of the debate was to refer the matter to a Committee of the Whole on the state of the Union. The House of Representatives did not constitute itself as a Committee of the Whole for this purpose until towards the end of the following month. Even so, the outcome of the debate of June 8, 1789 may be considered a victory for Madison and others who supported amendments. The debate concerned itself to a large extent with the question of whether it was advisable to consider amendments at all. It was followed by other debates, some of them long and fierce, but the later debates were more about the implementation of the decision of June 8, 1789, and particularly about the precise formulation of amendments and about where to attach them. By contrast, the question of principle, whether it was advisable to consider amendments at all, was not discussed in later debates in the protracted way that it was in the first debate. To judge by the content of the later debates, the necessity of amendments was by then conceded even by opponents. This may be the most important result of the debate of June 8, 1789.

Chapter 2 of this volume lays out the context of the debate. The composition of the first United States House of Representatives will be discussed. The sequence of speeches in the debate will be outlined and some attention will also be paid to the question of what sources there are for information on the debate. This question arises because at that time transcripts of debates in the United States House of Representatives were not published in the same way that they are published today. (The Senate, indeed, met in secret at that time.)

Chapter 3 takes up the subject of argumentation in the debate. Madison presented his proposals for amendments in the debate, but because there was such vehement opposition to the proposals and especially to considering the amendments at that time, it seems appropriate to proceed by considering the "rhetoric of reaction." This means examining the different ways in which opponents tried to thwart Madison. For this purpose, Albert Hirschman's fairly recent book entitled *The Rhetoric of Reaction* provides a useful analytic framework, even though it is seen to need some supplementation.

Chapter 4 investigates the styles of argumentation used by the chief participants in the debate. Of the people on the pro-amendment side, Madison is the only conceivable choice. Of those on the anti-amendment side, Congressmen Jackson and Vining have been selected, being the most insistent and vociferous in their opposition to Madison at this time. An appendix to this chapter gives the texts of the first part of Madison's key speech and of Jackson's and Vining's first speeches in full, and also provides a brief outline of what happened subsequently.

Chapters 3 and 4 thus offer an analysis, from two points of view, of a real-life debate, or at least of the best record available of a real-life debate, from two points of view. In chapters 5 to 9 attention is turned to analyses of literature.

Chapter 5 discusses *To Autumn*, which has sometimes been taken to be the most perfect of the famous odes of John Keats. It is suggested that a linguistically oriented investigation, focussing on grammatical properties of verbs in the poem, can provide new insights helpful to an interpretation of this well-loved poem.

Chapters 6 to 8 have a focus on Shakespeare. The first of these takes up the Kent episode in Act I of *King Lear* and the Pauline episode in Act II of *The Winter's Tale*. It seems fruitful to consider the two episodes in conjunction because of a number of similarities between them. For instance, in both a king is challenged by a person of lower rank and there are parallels in the ways that the two kings react to the challenges. Methods of linguistic pragmatics, it is suggested, may elucidate Shakespeare's conception of the two episodes.

Chapter 7 introduces a theme that recurs in the following two chapters of the book. This is the use of case grammar in the analysis of literature. The possibilities of this approach are explored from the point of view of translating Shakespeare in chapters 7 and 8. In chapter 7 some major soliloquies in *Othello* are examined. Building on the case grammar analyses of these speeches provided in Rudanko (1993a), the task here is to compare two standard translations of the play into Finnish, from different historical periods, with the original and with each other, to find out to what extent the spread of the different case roles is preserved or changed in the translations, in comparison with the original, and to investigate the implications of case role analysis for an interpretation of the play.

In chapter 8 a very modern rendering of *Othello* into Finnish is considered. The text is not only a translation but a script. The rendering has been considered "popularizing," and the linguistic reflexes of this impression are investigated. Extracts from the rendering are also considered from the point of view of case grammar.

In chapter 9 case grammar is likewise used as a tool of analysis, but now the subject matter of analysis is an episode in Theodore Dreiser's *Sister Carrie*, his first classic novel, which some critics consider his best. The episode has been selected because it comes at a turning-point in the novel: up to that point Hurstwood, one of the main characters in the novel, had been a debonair saloon manager; after the scene comes his flight with Carrie, followed by his inexorable decline. The episode, it is argued, also speaks to issues important to Dreiser, such as his conception of the roles of determinism and free will.

The texts included in this investigation are all important or influential and worth studying, though for different reasons. As far as the American Bill of Rights is concerned, it is a major, perhaps even the major, American contribution to Western democracy, and today its importance is felt all over the civilized world. The positions of Shakespeare and of Keats within the canon of Western and even world literature need no amplification, and are only emphasized by being occasionally targeted by some critics seeking to cast doubt on them or on their status. The position of Dreiser within the same canon may not be quite as self-evident or established, but *Sister Carrie* is a good example of one of the many possible texts of recurrent interest from a literary point of view to which methods such as those developed in this volume might be applied, with a view to their further refinement.

Chapter 2

The Bill of Rights and the Debate of June 8, 1789

The Bill of Rights and its World-Wide Import

American culture does not merely reflect a European cultural heritage. Rather it has a distinctive and pioneering quality of its own. As John H. McElroy points out in his book on the origins of American culture: "The opinion that the Constitution of the United States of America is merely a transatlantic variant of the British constitution is an Anglophilic fantasy" (McElroy (1989, 63); on some aspects of British influence on the United States Constitution, see Rutland (1983, 5 ff.).) Further, regarding the important idea of equality, McElroy makes this comment on the direction of influence:

> European philosophers in the 1600s and 1700s wrote about the idea that human beings have equal worth by virtue of being born human beings. But during America's cultural formation in those centuries, belief in equality of birth was not enculturated behavior from generation to generation in Europe. And at the time of the first war between Britain and America (1775-83), social identities fixed by birth were as much in force in British culture as they were anywhere else in Europe, and

hierarchical group privileges were as real as they were on the European mainland ... Until the settlement of central North America in the early 1600s, there was no place in the world where middling and lower-class Europeans who believed in their equality with other human beings could form a new population and a new civilization based on that belief. One may well ask whether the idea of equality would ever have become credible and influential throughout the world, including the continent of Europe, if there had been no nation like America where, from generation to generation, unprecedented historical conditions allowed that idea to become enculturated through behavior among a large population. (McElroy (1989, 60 f.))

"Social identities fixed by birth" have indeed been part of European culture, in some parts of Europe more so than in others, and it is important to recognize that the direction of cultural influence as far as the idea and the practice of equality is concerned has to a large extent been from America to Europe, as McElroy emphasizes.

Nor is this the direction of cultural influence only. Today it is, all too often, the direction also of the free flow of information. Here is Bernard Levin writing in the London *Times* in 1991:

A week or so ago I saw a headline reading "Bank of England fights to keep BCCI enquiry papers". It referred to the swindled depositors who are trying to find out what happened to their money, and in such circumstances you might think that even a judge would immediately order such disclosure. Yes, *you* might think it, but not I; the Bank was judicially allowed to have the vital papers bowdlerised.

Madder and madder; that splendid organization, the Campaign for Freedom of Information, has just revealed disturbing facts about the tests for pollution from pharmaceutical plants in Britain—a matter, surely, that potentially concerns us all. Not so; the Campaign's revelation is prohibited on pain of two years' imprisonment. But the Campaign's leaders will not go to chokey; they got the information from the United States Freedom of Information Act, not from Britain. Americans, you see, are trusted by their government; we are not fit to know whether we are going to be poisoned.

The Campaign has revealed a wide range of such British information garnered from America; this month's broadsheet is devoted to the subject, and readers will begin to think that they are hallucinating, so ridiculous and so scandalous are the things Americans can tell us that we cannot be told by our own governors. (Levin (1991, 14))

The fact that Europeans have to rely on the United States Bill of Rights to obtain information about affairs in their own countries should be sobering to anyone in Europe who still may hold a condescending or patronizing attitude toward American culture and civilization. It also renders it difficult to accept European characterizations of American culture and civilization as immature. Cultural and political maturity surely entails that those in authority have the self-confidence to accept the proposition that individual human beings have basic and inalienable rights and liberties, including the freedom of information, and that such rights do not depend on the generosity of those who happen to be in power at any one time. American culture is young in years, but it grew up fast, to be, in this respect, probably the most mature of all major civilizations, past or present.

To a considerable extent, American laws that protect the rights and liberties of individuals ultimately trace their actual or conceptual origins to the Bill of Rights. It is that document probably more than any other that today protects the freedom of expression in the United States. James Madison, who is often called the father of the Bill of Rights, could not have foreseen in 1789 the full import that his proposals were to assume for Western civilization in later centuries. However, he did show that he was fully aware of the British Constitution, including the English Bill of Rights of 1689, and also of its limitations:

> In the declaration of rights which that country has established, the truth is, they have gone no further than to raise a barrier against the power of the Crown; the power of the Legislature is left altogether indefinite. Although I know whenever the great rights, the trial by jury, freedom of the press, or liberty of conscience, come in question in that body, the invasion of them is resisted by able advocates, yet their Magna Charta does not contain any one provision for the security of those rights, respecting which the people of America are most alarmed. The freedom of the press and rights of conscience, those choicest privileges of the people, are unguarded in the British Constitution. (Gales (1834, 436))

How American politicians could have undertaken such a step to secure the "choicest privileges of the people" and how this step could have been maintained is a miracle in itself. The miracle can only be understood when it is realized that in its formative years American culture was shaped by people who populated the land by choice rather than by accident of birth. Such self-selecting immigrants and their descendants approved and put into practice the Bill of Rights with its key provisions for individual rights and liberties some two hundred years ago. (On the concept of self-selecting immigration to the United States, and on how immigration to some other parts of the world was not self-selecting, see McElroy (1989, chapter 2).) Meanwhile, for a long time, European culture and civilization, especially on the continent of Europe, remained to a considerable extent focused on notions about the mystique of the state, emanating from Hegel and other continental philosophers. Such notions, especially when they were combined with, and fueled by, nationalism, as happened all too frequently in some parts of continental Europe, came to amount to little more than providing a convenient fig leaf for self-perpetuating authoritarianism and the denial of the most basic human rights, especially the freedom of information, to individual human beings.

Admittedly, the American Federal Bill of Rights, promulgated in 1791, did not immediately assume the role that it has today. In particular, it took time for its provisions to become secure from impairment by state laws and constitutions. (On this process, see Abraham ([1967] 1988, 38 ff.).) However, once this was achieved, the Bill of Rights, and especially its key provisions for the freedom of the Press, gradually took on its current significance. Today, the First Amendment is undoubtedly the icon of the freedom of information in the United States. It also serves to ensure the accountability of public officials, for accountability tends to go together with openness and freedom of expression.

In today's world, as illustrated by the extract quoted above from Bernard Levin's column, the influence of the American Bill of Rights extends far beyond the borders of the United States. The First Amendment acts, directly or indirectly, to protect freedom of information not only in the United States but also in the rest of the world, at least in those parts that are civilized enough not to deny their citizens the freedom to travel abroad. In a direct way, if information is available and can be published in the United States, it is hard for any bodies or individuals outside the United States to prevent it from becoming available and public knowledge elsewhere in the world. At a more indirect level, even the knowledge that there is freedom of information in the United States may inhibit those in other countries from acting who would otherwise seek to suppress information in their own countries.

The Context of the Debate

Turning now to a more detailed account of the origins and historical context of the Bill of Rights, it will be recalled that a Bill of Rights was proposed at the Constitutional Convention in Philadelphia in 1787. In particular, James Mason of Virginia and Elbridge Gerry of Massachusetts attempted to set up a committee to draw up a Bill of Rights. However, the motion ran into opposition from Roger Sherman (Rutland (1983, 116)) and "was unceremoniously rejected, not receiving the favorable vote of a single state" (Dumbauld (1957, 5)). Other efforts at the Convention to include at least some specific rights, such as freedom of the press, were likewise rejected.

In spite of the negative decisions of the Constitutional Convention, the issue of amendments and of a Bill of Rights continued to exercise people's minds, and in elections to the First Congress, the issue of amendments played a significant role. As Bowling (1990, 126 f.) puts it, there was "little that was national about the first congressional election aside from the issue of amendments to the Constitution."

Regarding positions taken on this issue, the general tendency was for Antifederalists to demand amendments and for Federalists to be cool or lukewarm toward them. At a more delicate level, it seems useful to make a distinction between two types of amendments (cf. Bowling (1990, 121, 125)). First, there were what may be called structural amendments, or alterations. These called for change in the structure of government, especially in the relation between the Federal and State levels of government in favor of the latter. In general, proposals for structural alterations were advocated by Antifederalists but opposed by Federalists. (Cf. Bowling (1990, 121-126) on moves to introduce structural amendments.) Second, there were what may be called procedural amendments. This term designates amendments guaranteeing individual freedoms such as the freedom of speech. Antifederalists were in general also supportive of such rights-related amendments, which were "the most important drawing card for the Antifederalist demand for amendments" (Bowling (1990, 126)). The position of Federalists on procedural amendments was not entirely uniform. Most had been initially hostile to such amendments. This had been the case for instance at the Constitutional Convention of 1787. After the Convention some of them had been shifting their position, while others remained adamant in their opposition (cf. Bowling (1990, 125-129)). Overall, the difference between Federalists and Antifederalists with respect to amendments at the time of the first congressional elections might be summed up as follows: "while some Federalists, when pressed, supported amendments, the Antifederalists promised to fight for them and constantly brought them up as an issue they knew the Federalists wished to avoid" (Bowling (1990, 128)).

The first elections to the US Congress were clearly won by Federalists. As regards the House of Representatives, where the business of amendments was to originate, it has been calculated that of the approximately sixty members, more than four fifths were Federalists (cf. Bowling (1990, 16-17)).

When the First Congress of the United States convened, the issue of amendments hung finely in the balance. James Madison, a Federalist, had earlier been an opponent of amendments, but by 1789 his position had shifted. While still wanting to have nothing to do with structural alterations, he had come to support amendments for a Bill of Rights. Why he changed his position in this respect is an interesting question, but one that can probably never be answered completely, for it seems impossible definitively to untangle the reasons for the change in his position. A number of factors, including his concern and worry about calls for a second Constitutional Convention, the failure of North Carolina and Rhode Island to join the Union, the prodding of his friend Thomas Jefferson, and strong pro-Bill of Rights sentiments in his home state of Virginia, probably all played some part, but the relative significance of each in Madison's mind is not easy to measure. (On the shift in Madison's thinking, see Bowling (1988, 231 f.).)

Whatever the precise mix of his motives, Madison, in his election campaign against James Monroe for a seat in the House of Representatives, expressed support for rights-related amendments. (On Madison's election campaign, see Rutland (1983, 195 f.).) When the new Congress convened, Madison, having been elected by a narrow majority, became the prime mover for a Bill of Rights. On May 4, 1789, only a few weeks after the first Congress had started work, he announced his intention at a session of the House of Representatives to introduce amendments at a later point in time. On June 8, 1789 he duly fulfilled his promise.

The Sequence of Speeches

At the beginning of the day's proceedings on June 8, 1789, Madison asked the House of Representatives to constitute itself as a Committee of the Whole, in accordance with the fifth article of the Constitution, in order to consider amendments. The debate on that day, so important to United States and world history, turned out to be extraordinarily intense and protracted. Its general mood is well captured by Robert Rutland: "Instead of rushing to support his proposals, Madison's fellow congressmen seemed in no hurry to take up the topic which had so recently stirred the Republic" (Rutland (1983, 200)).

To gauge the intensity of the debate and the depth of the opposition to Madison's motion, we should examine the record of the proceedings in Gales (1834, 424-450). Here is a synopsis of the debate, with the speakers' first names and affiliations (Federalist or Antifederalist) provided on the basis of Bowling (1990, 20-41). (In Gales (1834, 424-450)) some of the speeches are presented in the first person, others in the third person. This is the reason for the shifts in perspective in the quotations in the survey.)

James Madison (Federalist) moved that the House "do now resolve itself into a Committee of the Whole on the State of the Union; by which an opportunity will be given, to bring forward some propositions, which I have strong hopes will meet the unanimous approbation of this House, after the fullest discussion ..."

William Smith (Federalist, of South Carolina) was opposed to Madison's motion, and asked to delay the "consideration of amending the Government, before it is organized ..."

James Jackson (Federalist) was also opposed to Madison's motion. In a lengthy speech he argued for delaying the consideration of amendments, ending by proposing a delay till the beginning of March, 1790.

Benjamin Goodhue (Federalist) observed that the speaker who preceded was "opposed to the consideration of amendments altogether." While thinking it "proper to attend to the subject earlier," Goodhue also argued that "the present time" was "premature, inasmuch as we have other business before us."

Aedanus Burke (Antifederalist) "thought amendments to the Constitution necessary," but he suggested a postponement "for the present."

James Madison (Federalist) expressed understanding for James Jackson's position "because he is unfriendly to the object ... in contemplation." However, he could not see that those who wished amendments to be considered "at the present session" stood "on good ground" when asking for a postponement. He motivated and renewed his motion for going into a committee.

Roger Sherman (Federalist) was "willing to let the subject be introduced," but only for the purpose of receiving (Madison's) propositions. He questioned "if any alteration which can now be proposed would be an amendment, in the true sense of the word," and he had "strong objections to being interrupted in completing the more important business."

Alexander White (Federalist) stated, in part: "I shall vote in favor of going into a Committee of the Whole, and, after receiving the subject, shall be content to refer it to a special committee to arrange and report."

William Smith (Federalist, of South Carolina) observed that if he (Madison) "did not succeed, he was not to blame." As for his own position, he was "induced to join the gentleman" (Madison), but "merely to receive his propositions." After that he would move that "the important and pressing business of the Government prevents their entering upon that subject at present."

John Page (Federalist) spoke in favor of Madison's motion, voicing the view that if Congress did not act in accordance with it there would be doubt whether it meant "seriously to enter upon the subject."

John Vining (Federalist) argued at length against Madison's motion, concluding that he would vote against the motion.

James Madison (Federalist) stated his reasons for amendments and the amendments themselves at length. As for the method of proceeding, instead of a Committee of the House as a Whole, he now proposed "that a committee be appointed to consider of and report such amendments as ought to be proposed by Congress to the Legislatures of the States, to become, if ratified by three-fourths thereof, part of the Constitution of the United States."

James Jackson (Federalist) was anything but impressed by Madison's long speech. He saw himself confirmed in his opposition to amendments: "The more I consider the subject of amendments, the more I am convinced it is improper."

Elbridge Gerry (Antifederalist) opined that going into a Committee of the Whole would be treating the subject "with the dignity its importance requires." He argued at length against referring the business to a special committee.

Samuel Livermore (Federalist) was against Madison's motion: "He was well satisfied in his own mind, that the people of America did not look for amendments at present."

Roger Sherman (Federalist) observed of the Constitution that "of the eleven States who have received it, the majority have ratified it without proposing a single amendment." Later on, he said: "It seems to be the opinion of gentlemen generally that this is not the time for entering upon the discussion of amendments: our only question therefore is, how to get rid of the subject."

Elbridge Gerry (Antifederalist) made the motion "that the business lie over until the 1st day of July next, and that it be the order for that day."

Thomas Sumter (Antifederalist) was "seriously inclined to give this subject a full discussion," but did "not wish it to be fully entered into at present."

John Vining (Federalist) opposed "the consideration of even proper alterations at this time." He "was against committing the subject to a select committee; if it were to be committed at all, he preferred a Committee of the Whole, but he hoped the subject would be postponed."

James Madison (Federalist) moved the propositions he had stated before and said that the House might do what they thought proper with them. "He accordingly moved the propositions by way of resolutions to be adopted by the House."

Samuel Livermore (Federalist) "objected to these propositions, because they did not take up the amendments of the several States."

John Page (Federalist) "was much obliged to his colleague [Madison, J.R.] for bringing the subject forward in the manner he had done."

John Lawrence (Federalist) "moved to refer Mr. Madison's motion to the Committee of the Whole on the State of the Union."

R. B. Lee (Federalist) supported taking it up in that committee, and "hoped his colleague would bring the propositions before the committee, when on the state of the Union, as he had originally intended."

Elias Boudinot (Federalist) "wished the appointment of a select committee, but afterwards withdrew his motion."

"At length Mr. LAWRENCE's motion was agreed to, and Mr. MADISON's propositions were ordered to be referred to a Committee of the Whole. Adjourned." (Gales (1834, 424-451); the attribution of the second speech to William Smith of South Carolina, rather than to William Smith of Maryland, is on the basis of *The Gazette of the United States*, June 10, 1789.)

The record of the debate in Gales (1834) fills over twenty columns of densely printed text. As far as its status as a source is concerned, it may be noted that it was "compiled from authentic materials" (Gales

(1834, title page)). Admittedly, it was published some 45 years after the event, and it is worth comparing the account given in Gales (1834) and summarized above with newspaper accounts of the debate that were published more or less immediately afterwards. The need for a comparison of this kind is accentuated by the consideration that Gales (1834) cannot always be considered a perfectly accurate source of information on proceedings of the House when it considered amendments (cf. Bowling (1990, 380)).

With respect to the present debate, two accounts of it in the press have been consulted, those in *The Gazette of the United States,* of June 10, 1789, and in *The Providence Gazette and Country Journal,* of June 20, 1789. These newspaper accounts are substantially the same, to the extent that it is possible to compare these, taken together, on the one hand, with the account in Gales (1834), on the other. (For other newspaper accounts on the same lines as the two mentioned, see those in *The Herald of Freedom and the Federal Advertiser,* June 16, 1789, and in *The American Herald and the Worcester Recorder,* of June 25, 1789. See also the accounts of the debate in Veit, Bowling, and Bickford (1991, 63-95).)

The newspaper accounts are substantially shorter than that given by Gales (1834). For instance, several of the speeches that come after Gerry's first speech in Gales (1834) have been omitted and summarized as "Several other gentlemen spoke upon the subject." This remark in the newspapers appears to cover the speeches by Livermore, Sherman, Gerry, Sumter, and Vining given in Gales (1834). Madison's fourth speech, coming next, is reported in both sources, followed by a speech by Samuel Livermore. From this point to the end of the debate there are some discrepancies between Gales (1834) and the newspaper accounts concerning the number and sequence of speeches, and in one or two cases even their content. It may therefore be best to present an alternative synopsis of this part of the debate based on the newspaper reports, starting with Madison's fourth speech:

> James Madison "withdrew his last motion for a select committee, and then submitted to the House a resolve comprizing a number of amendments to be incorporated in the constitution; these he read for the consideration of the House."
> Samuel Livermore "was opposed to this resolve—he conceived it entirely improper for any individual member to propose any particular number of amendments which do not take up the different amendments proposed by the several States."

John Page and R. B. Lee "severally rose to justify Mr. Madison; they thought themselves under great obligations to him, and conceived that the mode adopted was just and fair—and calculated to bring the attention of the House to a proper point in determining the subject."

James Madison said that "the subject should be brought forward in some form or another; ... he had thought proper to propose the form now submitted to the House." Further, he stated that "the resolve is now before the House, and they may do what they think proper with it."

John Lawrance "moved, that the resolve introduced by Mr. Madison, should be submitted to the consideration of a committee of the whole on the state of the Union."

Elias Boudinot "proposed a select committee to consist of a member from each State."

"After a few more observations, the motion of Mr. LAWRANCE being put was carried in the affirmative.—The House then adjourned." (*The Gazette of the United States,* June 10, 1789)

Some discrepancies are found, then, between the account in Gales (1834) and the picture presented by the newspaper reports, especially with regard to the latter stages of the debate. There is for instance the question of the precise position of R. B. Lee's speech in the sequence of speeches: in the newspaper accounts it comes before John Laurance's motion, whereas in Gales (1834) it comes after it. (The spelling of John Laurance's surname varies in the sources, but this variation will be set aside. Apart from quotations, which will not be modified, the spelling "Laurance," based on Bowling (1990, 27), will be used here.) Further, as far as the end of the debate is concerned, the newspaper accounts report a vote on Mr. Laurance's motion, a possible interpretation being that the vote was between Mr. Laurance's motion "that the resolve introduced by Mr. Madison, should be submitted to the consideration of a committee of the whole on the state of the Union" and Mr. Boudinot's motion for a select committee that came at the very end of the debate. By contrast, according to the record in Gales (1834), Mr. Boudinot withdrew his motion and the phrasing in Gales (1834) "At length Mr. LAWRENCE's motion was agreed to" does not specifically mention a vote, though it is compatible with it.

Such discrepancies seem hard to resolve completely at this distance in time and do need to be borne in mind. However, they appear to be of a fairly minor nature. For instance, in the case of the speech by R. B. Lee just mentioned, while there is a discrepancy with respect to its precise position in the sequence of speeches, both records agree that this member spoke in support of considering Madison's proposals. As regards the conclusion of the debate, it would certainly be useful to obtain more specific information on the finale and on whether the newspapers are correct in reporting a vote at the end of the proceedings, and if so, it would be highly desirable to know which motions were voted on and how the vote went. However, this is not so much a question of a factual discrepancy between the two accounts as of a gap in reporting aspects of what happened at the end of the debate, and the evidence of both records shows clearly enough that the conclusion of the debate was the adoption of Mr. Laurance's motion to refer Madison's propositions to the Committee of the Whole of the State of the Union.

Overall, then, while some discrepancies between Gales (1834) and contemporary accounts of the debate must be acknowledged, their significance should not be exaggerated. The consideration of the evidence of contemporary newspaper accounts here was necessarily restricted in scope, but it seems in the light of it that the account of the debate of June 8, 1789 in Gales (1834) is accurate in major respects. This holds especially of the first fourteen speeches in the debate, up to and including Gerry's first speech. As far as these fourteen speeches are concerned, the identities of the speakers are exactly the same in both sources, and the same is true of the sequential order of the speakers. The contents of the speeches are also substantially the same, though the newspaper accounts tend to be more compressed. This compression may well be at least partly dictated by the requirements of the medium, which may also explain the hiatus in the newspaper accounts observed after Gerry's first speech; the hiatus does not call into question the account of the five speeches in Gales (1834). The discrepancies in the final part of the debate are more noteworthy, but they still concern only nuances of reporting and do not call into question anything substantive in the more comprehensive account in Gales (1834). Under these circumstances, it seems best to use Gales (1834) as the principal source of the discussion here.

The referral of Madison's propositions to a committee represented a victory for Madison. Of the other motions made during the debate, James Jackson's motion to delay consideration of the matter to March 1, 1790, that is, by some nine months, would have represented a serious setback. Some other speakers proposed an indefinite delay, with John Vining concluding his second speech: "if it [Madison's motion, J.R.] was to be committed at all, he preferred a Committee of the

Whole, but hoped the subject would be postponed" (Gales (1834, 449)). If the House of Representatives had refused to commit Madison's motion to a committee or had delayed consideration of the matter till the spring of 1790 or indeed indefinitely, it is impossible to say whether the proposals could ever have been resurrected in the first Congress — or whether the first Congress would even have had the time to consider them. And if the proposals had not been considered in the first Congress, it is likewise impossible to speculate on what might have happened in the second Congress and on whether the passage of time would have helped or hindered the cause of such a fundamental readjustment of the Constitution as the amendments represented. After all, with time passing, the new nation might have come to manage without a Bill of Rights, as have other countries that lack such a code to this day.

The adoption of Laurance's motion was a victory for the cause of the Bill of Rights, but the debate that preceded was intense, with Madison facing stiff and determined opposition. It is hard to overestimate Madison's role in the debate on the pro-amendment side. He spoke four or five times, more often than any other member, and his perseverance kept the debate going, in the face of criticism and opposition from both sides. Antifederalists were not particularly keen on Madison's propositions, since it was clear enough that they did not favor structural alterations and instead focused on rights-related amendments. As for Federalists, they had the overwhelming majority of seats in the first House of Representatives, and their opposition was a very serious matter. A degree of opposition was no doubt to be expected, in view of the long-standing Federalist coolness toward, or ambivalence on, amendments, but the scope and intensity of the resistance displayed in the debate may well have been a surprise even to Madison. In the course of the debate Federalist opponents such as James Jackson and Roger Sherman made no secret of their confidence in the strength of their side, with Jackson going as far as claiming in his second speech that the "sense of the House" was against considering "the business of amendments" "until next Spring" (Gales (1834, 444) and Sherman suggesting in a similar vein that the "only question" was "how to get rid of the subject" (Gales (1834, 448)). How Madison's propositions survived under such circumstances is almost a miracle and remains a question that invites investigation. A consideration of the types and the styles of argumentation used in the debate offers a handle on one aspect of how the miracle came about.

Chapter 3

Rhetoric of Reaction in the Debate of June 8, 1789

This examination of the "rhetoric of reaction" used in the debate of June 8, 1789 will take as its point of departure the analytic framework developed by Albert Hirschman for the study of political argumentation in his book *The Rhetoric of Reaction*, published in 1991. The framework relates specifically to the different ways in which opponents of change may respond to fresh ideas and new initiatives in order to thwart change and preserve the status quo. According to Hirschman, there are three such general "reactive-revolutionary theses": the "*perversity thesis* or thesis of the perverse effect," the "*futility thesis,*" and the "*jeopardy thesis.*"

The perversity thesis holds that "any purposive action to improve some feature of the political, social, or economic order only serves to exacerbate the condition one wishes to remedy" (Hirschman (1991, 7)). Hirschman illustrates this thesis for instance by the argumentation used by opponents of the establishment of the Poor Laws in nineteenth-century England: "the availability of the assistance, so it was argued, acts as a positive encouragement to 'sloth' and 'depravity' and thus *produces* poverty instead of relieving it" (Hirschman (1991, 29); emphasis in the original). It has also been argued in a more modern context, of course, that policies of public assistance to the poor may only cause those on low wages to stop working and induce them to live on public assistance, with the same result of producing rather than relieving poverty (cf. Hirschman (1991, 34 f.)).

According to the futility thesis, "attempts at social transformation will be unavailing" (Hirschman (1991, 7)). Or, in a more fully articulated form, the thesis holds "that the attempt at change is abortive, that in one way or another any alleged change is, was, or will be largely surface, facade, cosmetic, hence illusory, as the 'deep' structures of society remain wholly untouched" (Hirschman (1991, 43)). Hirschman (1991, 48 f.) illustrates the futility thesis for instance by reference to de Tocqueville's assessment of the French Revolution, which deflated the supposedly pivotal character of this event.

The jeopardy thesis holds that "the proposed change, though perhaps desirable in itself, involves unacceptable costs or consequences of one sort or another" (Hirschman (1991, 81)). In a more narrow sense, the thesis can be seen as relating a new reform to an older reform: "... the reactionary takes on once again the progressive's clothes and argues as though both the new and the old progress were desirable, and then shows typically how a new reform, if carried out, would mortally *endanger* an older, highly prized one that, moreover, may have only recently been put into place. The older hard-won conquests or accomplishments cannot be taken for granted and would be placed in jeopardy by the new program" (Hirschman (1991, 84); emphasis in the original). In this connection Hirschman considers arguments against widening suffrage in nineteenth century England on the grounds that this might endanger the liberty of citizens.

Hirschman's illustrations of his theses derive mainly from broad intellectual and political debates. References to actual debates in European parliaments do occur but are less prominent. Discussions of debates in the United States Congress are still more rare. There is no discussion at all in Hirschman's book of the American Bill of Rights or of the applicability of his theses to the debates that preceded its adoption. It is therefore of interest to see to what extent the three theses may be applied to the debate of June 8, 1789. The starting position of such an inquiry seems to fit Hirschman's premises, since the point of the debate was to consider something that was clearly an innovation, so that there was a well-defined dichotomy between the positions of those wishing change and of those wishing to preserve the status quo.

An application of the analytic tools of the rhetoric of reaction to the debate of June 8, 1789 reveals that major aspects of what the opponents of Madison's motions had to say can indeed be explicated with reference to Hirschman's three theses. Some examples are worth adducing, in order both to illustrate the applicability of the theses and to throw light on the particular form of each thesis in the debate and on the relations of the theses to each other.

As far as the perversity thesis is concerned, in this debate it takes the form of the argument that even though amendments are submitted for the purpose of safeguarding individual freedoms, the outcome of such a proposal is to make the freedoms in question less secure. This is a daring intellectual maneuver and it is not very prominent in the debate, but it does surface. In particular, in his second speech James Jackson observes:

> There is a maxim in law, and it will apply to bills of rights, that when you enumerate exceptions, the exceptions operate to the exclusion of all circumstances that are omitted; consequently, unless you except every right from the grant of power, those omitted are inferred to be resigned to the discretion of the Government. (Gales (1834, 442))

Later on in the same speech Jackson adds that "... those who now clamor for alterations, may, ere long, discover that they have marred a good Government, and rendered their own liberties insecure" (Gales (1834, 444)).

A possible reason for the relative absence of the perversity argument in the debate is that it was tackled head-on by Madison. At one point in his third speech he observed:

> It has been objected also against a bill of rights, that, by enumerating particular exceptions to the grant of power, it would disparage those rights which were not placed in that enumeration; and it might follow by implication, that those rights which were not singled out, were intended to be assigned into the hands of the General Government, and were consequently insecure. This is one of the most plausible arguments I have ever heard urged against the admission of a bill of rights into this system; but, I conceive, it may be guarded against. I have attempted it, as gentlemen may see by turning to the last clause of the fourth resolution. (Gales (1834, 439))

And in the last clause of the fourth resolution, Madison proposed what can only be considered the perfect response to the present perversity argument:

> The exceptions here or elsewhere in the Constitution, made in favor

of particular rights, shall not be so construed as to diminish the just importance of other rights retained by the people, or as to enlarge the powers delegated by the Constitution; but either as actual limitations of such powers, or as inserted merely for greater caution. (Gales (1834, 435))

Madison's phrasing is slightly wordy, but the value of the clause in question is reflected in the fact that its basic idea underlies article X of the Federal Bill of Rights, as promulgated on December 15, 1791 (Rutland (1983, 245)):

The powers not delegated to the United States by the Constitution, nor prohibited by it to the States, are reserved to the States respectively, or to the people.

It seems fair to claim, on the basis of the overall content of James Jackson's speeches on June 8, 1789, that his use of the perversity thesis was intended to set his fellow members of the House of the Representatives against considering Madison's amendments. However, almost paradoxically, or perversely, the use of the thesis, anticipated and met head-on by Madison, led to a more sophisticated formulation of Madison's propositions.

As far as the futility thesis is concerned, in the present context it amounts to the claim that Madison's amendments will have no effect if they are enacted and are therefore unnecessary. The thesis surfaces in a number of the speeches of Madison's opponents. Thus Roger Sherman asks rhetorically: "Now, will gentlemen give up these points to go into a discussion of amendments, when no advantage can arise from them?" He goes on: "For my part, I question if any alteration which can now be proposed would be an amendment, in the true sense of the word ..." (Gales (1834, 428)). Also arguing along the lines of the futility thesis, James Jackson claims that the proposed amendments are unnecessary since what they are purported to achieve has already been achieved. Thus he says in his second speech:

But do gentlemen suppose bills of rights necessary to secure liberty? If they do, let them look at New York, New Jersey, Virginia, South Carolina, and Georgia. Those States have no bill of rights, and is the liberty of the citizens less safe in those States, than in the other of the United States? I believe it is not. (Gales (1834, 442))

And slightly later in the same speech he goes on:

> The gentleman endeavors to secure the liberty of the press; prey how is this in danger? There is no power given to Congress to regulate this subject as they can commerce, or peace, or war. Has any transaction taken place to make us suppose such an amendment necessary? (Gales (1834, 442))

Madison did not attempt to reply to all such rhetorical questions: he had in fact anticipated Jackson's version of the futility argument in these measured tones:

> It has been said, by way of objection to a bill of rights, ... that they are unnecessary articles of a Republican Government, upon the presumption that the people have those rights in their own hands, and that is the proper place for them to rest. It would be a sufficient answer to say, that this objection lies against such provisions under the State Governments, as well as under the General Government; and there are, I believe, but few gentlemen who are inclined to push their theory so far as to say that a declaration of rights in those cases is either ineffectual or improper. (Gales (1834, 437 f.))

Another possible variant of the futility thesis might be that a bill of rights is useless because its provisions would not take effect, it being the case that not all State bills of rights have always been observed. This variant does not figure prominently in the speeches of anti-amendment speakers in the debate, but Madison addresses it:

> It has been said that it is unnecessary to load the Constitution with this provision, because it was not found effectual in the constitution of the particular States. It is true, there are a few particular States in which some of the most valuable articles have not, at one time or other, been violated; but it does not follow but they may have, to a certain degree, a salutary effect against the abuse of power. If they are incorporated into the Constitution, independent tribunals of justice will consider themselves in a peculiar manner the guardians of those rights; they will be an impenetrable bulwark against every assumption of power in the Legislative or Executive; ... (Gales (1834, 439))

There is a further line of argument surfacing in the debate that bears a relation to the futility thesis, even though, strictly speaking, it is not an instance of it. We may consider these remarks by Roger Sherman:

It is a wonder that there has been so much unanimity in adopting it [the Constitution, J.R.], considering the ordeal it had to undergo; and the unanimity which prevailed at its formation is equally astonishing; amidst all the members from the twelve States present at the Federal Convention, there were only three who did not sign the instrument to attest their opinion of its goodness. Of the eleven States who have received it, the majority have ratified it without proposing a single amendment. This circumstance leads me to suppose that we shall not be able to propose any alterations that are likely to be adopted by nine States; and gentlemen know, before the alterations take effect, they must be agreed to by the Legislatures of three-fourths of the States in the Union. Those States which have not recommended alterations will hardly adopt them, unless it is clear that they tend to make the Constitution better. Now, how this can be made out to their satisfaction I am yet to learn; they know of no defect from experience. (Gales (1834, 447-448))

The idea here might be described as the "vicarious rejection" or the "vicarious impediment" thesis: it is futile for the institution that is debating an initiative to change the status quo to propose a change, because in order to take effect the proposed change will need to be approved by another institution and that other institution will be unlikely to approve the initiative. This thesis does not fall under the futility thesis proper, since the futility thesis holds that the "alleged change is, was, or will be largely surface, facade, cosmetic, hence illusory," that is, the thesis concerns the futility of the content of the change. The vicarious rejection thesis, by contrast, concerns more the procedure, and not so much the content, of the change. Nonetheless, even the vicarious rejection scenario involves a sense of futility, the futility of spending time on something that is doomed.

Any amendments of course also needed to be approved not only by the requisite number of States but also by the Senate. From this angle, we will not be surprised to see a reference to deliberations of that body offered as a reason for not accepting Madison's motion. Samuel Livermore duly argued along these lines in his first speech. We may quote the report in Gales (1834):

He wished the concurrence of the Senate upon entering on this business, because if they opposed the measure, all the House did would be mere waste of time; and there was some little difficulty on this point, because it required the consent of two-thirds of both Houses to agree to what was proper on this occasion. (Gales (1834, 447))

Madison was equal to the vicarious rejection argument. In his third speech he observed:

> And in this case it is necessary to proceed with caution; for while we feel all these inducements to go into a revisal of the Constitution, we must feel for the Constitution itself, and make that revisal a moderate one. I should be unwilling to see a door opened for a reconsideration of the whole structure of the Government—for a re-consideration of the principles and the substance of the powers given; because I doubt, if such a door were opened, we should be very likely to stop at that point which would be safe to the Government itself. But I do wish to see a door opened to consider, so far as to incorporate those provisions for the security of rights, against which I believe no serious objection has been made by any class of our constituents: such as would be likely to meet with the concurrence of two-thirds of both Houses, and the approbation of three-fourths of the State Legislatures. I will not propose a single alteration which I do not wish to see take place, as intrinsically proper in itself, or proper because it is wished for by a respectable number of my fellow-citizens; and therefore I shall not propose a single alteration but is likely to meet the concurrence required by the Constitution. (Gales (1834, 432-433))

When dealing with the vicarious rejection thesis, Madison thus distinguished between two types of amendments, the distinction corresponding, at least to a very large extent, to that made in the previous chapter between "structural" and "procedural" (or rights-related) amendments. He emphasized, with an eye to his fellow Federalists, that structural alterations were not to be contemplated. This reassurance had some effect on one of the opponents, John Vining, whose observations in his second speech are reported, in part, as follows:

> There were many things mentioned by some of the State Conventions which he would never agree to, on any conditions whatever; they changed the principles of the Government, and were therefore obnoxious to its friends. The honorable gentleman from Virginia had not touched upon any of them; he was glad of it, because he could by no means bear the idea of an alteration respecting them; he referred to the mode of obtaining direct taxes, judging of elections, &c. (Gales (1834, 449))

With structural alterations, of the kind Vining mentioned, set aside by Madison, the rights-related amendments that were proposed and that deserved discussion had, by contrast, every chance, according to Madison, of being accepted in the Senate and the State Legislatures. This meant that the vicarious rejection thesis was not valid and that members of the House of Representatives were not wasting their time discussing his propositions.

Yet another type of obstructionist move bears some indirect relation to the futility thesis. Here is an extract from James Jackson's first speech:

> Much has been said by the opponents to this Constitution, respecting the insecurity of jury trials, that great bulwark of personal safety. All their objections may be done away, by proper regulations on this point, and I do not fear but such regulations will take place. The bill is now before the Senate, and a proper attention is shown to this business. Indeed, I cannot conceive how it could be opposed; I think an almost omnipotent Emperor would not be hardy enough to set himself against it. (Gales (1834, 425-6))

The thesis here might be dubbed that of "vicarious agency" or of "unnecessary duplication": to the extent that there is merit in the measure being considered by the present institution (the House of Representatives), another institution (the Senate) is in the process of formulating a law to solve the problem. That is, what the present institution is doing now is unnecessary because another institution is doing the job. This thesis may be used to block change: if the present institution fails to consider a measure on these grounds, it may turn out that the other body may later decide not to do the job either. Or, more directly, the thesis may be used to block or impede change because the present institution may be prevailed upon to wait for the results of the deliberations of the other institution. This line of reasoning is implicit in James Jackson's speech and it also surfaces briefly in John Vining's first speech:

> And here let me ask gentlemen how they propose to amend that part of the Constitution which embraces the judicial branch of the Government, when they do not know the regulations proposed by the Senate, who are forming a bill on this subject? (Gales (1834, 430))

This thesis of vicarious agency is another procedural argument. It comes up once or twice in the debate under review, but is not very prominent, no doubt because a full bill of rights was not under consideration elsewhere at the time.

Turning now to the jeopardy thesis, we recall that using it, an opponent of change argues that "a new reform, if carried out, would mortally *endanger* an older, highly prized one that, moreover, may have only recently been put in place" (Hirschman (1991, 84); emphasis in the original). Here the reform to have "only recently been put in place" is the United States Constitution, and there are those in the debate who saw Madison endangering that reform. Here is James Jackson again:

> But in what a situation shall we be with respect to those foreign Powers with whom we desire to be in treaty? They look upon us as a nation emerging into figure and importance. But what will be their opinion, if they see us unable to retain the national advantages we have just gained? They will smile at our infantile efforts to obtain consequence, and treat us with the contempt we have hitherto borne by reason of the imbecility of our Government. Can we expect to enter into a commercial competition with any of them, while our system is incomplete? And how long it will remain in such a situation, if we enter upon amendments, God only knows. Our instability will make us objects of scorn. We are not content with two revolutions in less than fourteen years; we must enter upon a third, without necessity or propriety. Our faith will be like the *punica fides* of Carthage; and we shall have none that will repose confidence in us. (Gales (1834, 443))

Jackson's is a foreign policy argument: considering amendments will call into question the stability brought about by the Constitution that has only recently come into force. Such constitutional instability, in turn, would reduce the emerging international stature of the country. This excursion into foreign relations in the debate did not elicit a direct response from Madison or his followers. Nor did Madison's opponents take up Jackson's point.

Above, a large number of objections to Madison's motion have been considered and illustrated. Hirschman's model has been seen to be a useful analytic tool for the analysis of the debate in question. However, the most generally occurring objection to Madison's motion has not been explicitly introduced as yet. This might be summed up as the thesis of timing: the present time is not right for considering Madison's motion.[1] This theme runs through a large number of the speeches of the opponents. The report on the speech of Aedanus Burke may serve as an example:

Mr. BURKE thought amendments to the Constitution necessary, but this was not the proper time to bring them forward. He wished the Government completely organized before they entered upon this ground. The law for collecting the revenue is immediately necessary; the Treasury Department must be established; till this, and other important subjects are determined, he was against taking this up. (Gales (1834, 426))

Almost inevitably, we should quote James Jackson again. Here is the conclusion to his first speech:

Let the Constitution have a fair trial; let it be examined by experience, discover by that test what its errors are, and then talk of amending; but to attempt it now is doing it at a risk, which is certainly imprudent. I have the honor of coming from a State that ratified the Constitution by the unanimous vote of a numerous convention: the people of Georgia have manifested their attachment to it, by adopting a State Constitution framed upon the same plan as this. But although they are thus satisfied, I shall not be against such amendments as will gratify the inhabitants of other States, provided they are judged of by experience and not merely on theory. For this reason, I wish the consideration of the subject postponed until the 1st of March, 1790. (Gales (1834, 426))

These two extracts have been chosen with the purpose of illustrating not only the thesis of timing but a distinction that should be made with respect to the thesis. The argument of timing is not always a ploy to thwart an initiative to change the status quo, and allowance must be made for speakers who had a genuine concern about attending to some other pressing business first, without wishing to use timing as an excuse to kill Madison's proposals. On the basis of the fairly well defined tasks that Burke wanted done first, and perhaps also because of his Antifederalist affiliation, it may be presumed that for him timing was not a tactic to thwart the motion. On the other hand, as far as James Jackson is concerned, it seems safe to conclude that in spite of his statement that he would not be against amendments under the conditions that he stated, this was a mere rhetorical ploy or an excuse to prevent amendments from being considered. The reason for this judgment is based on the totalities of his two speeches and also on the reactions of his Federalist colleagues. Benjamin Goodhue, speaking next, started by reacting to James Jackson:

I believe it would be perfectly right in the gentleman who spoke last, to move a postponement to the time he has mentioned; because he is opposed to the consideration of amendments altogether. (Gales (1834, 426))

And from the beginning of Madison's second speech we get confirmation that those employing the thesis of timing should indeed be divided into two groups and that Madison was aware of the division:

The gentleman from Georgia (Mr. Jackson) is certainly right in his opposition to my motion for going into a Committee of the Whole, because he is unfriendly to the object I have in contemplation; but I cannot see that the gentlemen who wish for amendments to be proposed at the present session, stand on good ground when they object to the House going into committee on this business. (Gales (1834, 426-427))

Turning to Madison's more general response to the thesis of timing, it may be observed that he warned his fellow Representatives of the dangers of postponing the consideration of amendments:

But if we continue to postpone from time to time, and refuse to let the subject come into view, it may occasion suspicions, which, though not well founded, may tend to inflame or prejudice the public mind against our decisions. They may think we are not sincere in our desire to incorporate such amendments in the Constitution as will secure those rights, which they consider as not sufficiently guarded. (Gales (1834, 427))

And John Page, one of Madison's very few hard-core supporters in the debate, expressed some of the dangers of postponement more bluntly in his first speech:

He [Madison, J.R.] has done me the honor of showing me certain propositions which he has drawn up; they are very important, and I sincerely wish the House may receive them. After they are published, I think the people will wait with patience till we are at leisure to resume them. But it must be very disagreeable to them to have it postponed from time to time, in the manner it has been for six weeks past; they will be tired out by fruitless expectation. Putting myself into the place of those who favor amendments, I should suspect Congress did not mean seriously to enter upon the subject; that it was vain to expect redress from them. I should begin to turn my attention to the alternative contained in the fifth article, and think of joining the Legislatures of those States which have applied for calling a new convention. How dangerous such an expedient would be I need not mention; but I venture to affirm, that unless you take early notice of this subject, you will not have power to deliberate. The people will clamor for a new convention; they will not trust the House any longer. Those, therefore, who dread the assembling of a convention, will do well to acquiesce in the present motion, and lay the foundation of a most important work. (Gales (1834, 429))

Madison's remarks and those of Page emphasize the risks and dangers inherent in not acting. They bring to mind what Hirschman (1991, 153) calls the "*imminent danger thesis.*" Hirschman views this as the opposite of the jeopardy thesis, but the two share some features:

First of all, both look at only one category of dangers or risks when a new program is discussed: the jeopardy camp will conjure up exclusively the dangers of action, whereas the imminent-danger partisans will wholly concentrate on the risks of inaction. [Note omitted, J.R.] Second, both camps present their respective scenarios—the harm that will come from either action or inaction—as though they were entirely certain and inescapable. (Hirschman (1991, 153))

The imminent danger thesis fits Madison's and Page's remarks fairly well, but it is not the only response that these Representatives have to the thesis of timing. Towards the end of his third speech, Madison observes in part: "I should advocate greater despatch in the business of amendments, if I were not convinced of the absolute necessity there is of pursuing the organization of the Government ..." (Gales (1834, 442)). That is, he took account of the thesis of timing by making the point that he was not advocating immediately giving over the legislative agenda to the consideration of amendments. A similar point is made by Page near the beginning of the speech just quoted. The response by the pro-amendment side to the thesis of timing was thus two-pronged, based on both the imminent danger thesis and a willingness to show a degree of flexibility regarding timing.

There is one more obstructionist thesis left, though it is probably less easily generalizable to other debates than most of the techniques considered so far. It surfaces in the second speech by William Smith (of South Carolina):

> Mr. SMITH, of South Carolina, thought the gentleman who brought forward the subject had done his duty: he had supported his motion with ability and candor, and if he did not succeed, he was not to blame. (Gales (1834, 429))

Much the same idea comes up even more forcefully at the very end of James Jackson's second speech:

> How are we then to extricate ourselves from this labyrinth of business? Certainly we shall lose much of our valuable time, without any advantage whatsoever. I hope, therefore, the gentleman [Madison, J.R.] will press us no further; he has done his duty, and acquitted himself of the obligation under which he lay. He may now accede to what I take to be the sense of the House, and let the business of amendments lie over until next Spring; that will be soon enough to take it up to any good purpose. (Gales (1834, 444))

The point of these speakers here is that Madison had done his duty and had carried out the obligation that he had undertaken. This, no doubt, refers to Madison's campaign pledge when running for his seat in the House of Representatives. Madison does not dignify this point with an answer, and it should have become clear by now that Madison was not introducing amendments in order to go through the motions of fulfilling a campaign pledge.

The obstructionist technique in question here is hard to sum up with one word. It may perhaps be called the "obligations honored" thesis. Even though this technique presupposes rather special circumstances, in particular, a previous undertaking given, this does not mean that it cannot be used in other debates. Wherever the person or persons proposing something have been prompted or induced to promise to make the proposal in question in order to achieve some other end, perhaps to get elected, the technique is available to opponents when the time comes to redeem the pledge. Under such circumstances, the person or persons in question may indeed be expected not to persist too much in their proposal, since it may have been neither their own nor in accordance with their own true inclinations in the first place. However, in the present debate it is impossible to call Madison's commitment and his perseverance into question.

To sum up, the investigation carried out in this chapter has served a two-fold purpose. First, with respect to Hirschman's theses, it has shown how the theses might usefully be supplemented. In particular, the discussion has identified the theses of vicarious rejection and of vicarious agency as procedural moves that may be used to obstruct the consideration of a measure in the body which is currently considering it. Further, the discussion has highlighted the importance that may attach to arguments of timing and how the thesis of timing may be used as an obstructionist technique. An ostensible concern about timing on the part of a speaker may be used to mask the speaker's hostility to the measure as such. This is undoubtedly what happens in James Jackson's first speech, but the maneuver is spotted immediately by Goodhue and Madison, no doubt on the basis of their real-world knowledge of their colleague. Where such knowledge is lacking, the tactic, it may be speculated, may well work better.

A second objective of this investigation was to examine what light Hirschman's theses throw on argumentation in a concrete and well-defined debate. Here it would appear that Hirschman's theses, provided that they are supplemented with the additional theses outlined and illustrated above, do indeed reveal the rhetorical richness of the obstructionist techniques used in the debate and the ingenuity of the speakers. The discussion has also served to substantiate the sense that on the obstructionist side James Jackson was the most inventive and ingenious speaker, as far as reactionary rhetoric is concerned. His arsenal of obstructionist techniques in the debate was an impressively rich one. One is almost hard put to find a technique that he did not use. On the pro-amendment side, the outstanding figure was of course Madison himself. The discussion has also served to show the depth of his contribution. The discussion of the different reactionary and obstructionist theses demonstrates that he was not just going through the motions of fulfilling a campaign pledge. He anticipated and answered the most varied modes of obstruction employed in the debate and in him James Jackson met his superior. The present investigation serves to show some of the ways in which it was in large measure thanks to Madison's skill and perseverance on June 8, 1789 that Western civilization was enriched with the United States Bill of Rights.

Notes to Chapter 3

1. The thesis of timing, "the Time is not Ripe," is mentioned by F. M. Cornford in his at least partly jocular or tongue-in-cheek brochure *Microcosmographia Academica,* as observed in passing by Hirschman (1991, 83). In a brief paragraph Cornford ([1908] 1953, 16) uses the label "the Principle of Unripe Time" to designate a type of argument for doing nothing. The paragraph in question runs as follows:

> Another argument is that *'the Time is not Ripe.'* The Principle of Unripe Time is that people should not do at the present moment what they think right at that moment, because the moment at which they think it right has not yet arrived. But the unripeness of the time will, in some cases, be found to lie in the Bugbear, 'What Dr ——— will say.' Time, by the way, is like the medlar; it has a trick of going rotten before it is ripe. (Cornford ([1908] 1953, 16))

Chapter 4

Rhetorical Styles in the Debate of June 8, 1789

Chapter 3 focused on the content of argumentation in the debate of June 8, 1789. The present chapter will turn to the rhetorical styles of leading protagonists on either side. As far as the small number of speakers in the pro-Bill of Rights group is concerned, Madison himself is the only conceivable choice. As observed in chapters 2 and 3, he provided the impetus for the debate and spoke several times in the course of it. His central speech was the one in which he presented his amendments. In the early part of this speech he motivated his amendments before formulating them and also spelled out his reasons why in the first place he wanted to introduce the question of amendments at that time. This early part will be considered in more detail below.

As far as the opposing side is concerned, no one speaker stands out alone in the debate quite to the same extent as Madison does on his side. However, there seems little doubt, on the basis of the variety and ingenuity of argumentation as demonstrated in chapter 3, that James Jackson was the most prominent and the most vociferous among the opponents. It is not for nothing that William Foster, in a biography, dubbed Jackson "the chief opponent of the first efforts to amend the Constitution" (Foster (1960, 74)).

James Jackson will here be paired with John Vining. Vining too spoke twice in the course of the debate. His objection to Madison's motion clearly ran deeper at this time than concern about the timing of a debate on amendments, for in his second speech in the debate he observed "that a bill of rights was unnecessary in a Government deriving all its powers from the people" (Gales (1834, 449)). (On Vining's later role, see Rutland (1983, 207).) The selection of speeches for consideration here, by Madison, on the one hand, and by Jackson and Vining, on the other, is motivated by the desire to take account of the major contributions of the main protagonists on either side of the debate of June 8, 1789.

Speeches by Opponents

We will first consider Jackson's and Vining's first speeches. As became clear in the previous chapter, their substance may be explicated with the help of theses of reactionary rhetoric. Here, however, we will be concerned with the rhetorical styles of the two speeches. They share some significant features. One of these is the relatively large number of *let* imperatives. In Jackson's speech we have the following:

> Let us, gentlemen, fit our vessel, set up her masts, and expand her sails, and be guided by the experiment in our alterations.
> But let me ask what will be the consequence of taking up this subject?
> Let the Constitution have a fair trial; let it be examined by experience, ... (Gales (1834, 425 f.))

The following examples are taken from Vining's speech:

> True; but, say gentlemen, let us go into committee; ...
> And here let me ask gentlemen how ...
> ... let him take the mode I have mentioned, ... (Gales (1834, 429-430))

Such imperatives are well represented in both speeches. However, the rhetorical figure which is the most important in each is the rhetorical question, and it is this, therefore, which will be the subject of closer attention here.

A first definition of rhetorical questions is to say that they are questions "that don't expect an answer" (Hudson (1975, 16)). Or rhetorical questions are characterized by "the fact that the answer is a foregone conclusion" (Quirk et al. (1985, 1478)). Such characterizations are helpful, but to get a better purchase on the concept, it seems useful to approach it both from a grammatical and from an illocutionary point of view. It is not always easy to keep these points of view entirely separate, but distinguishing them will help to structure the present discussion. As far as grammatical properties are concerned, the division of ordinary or regular (non-rhetorical) questions into *yes-no* questions (for instance, see Bolinger (1978)) and *wh* questions extends to the analysis of rhetorical questions, as has been noted. (See Pope (1976, 36-46) for a standard grammatical analysis; for one or two elaborations, see Rudanko (1993b).)

Here are two of Pope's examples of rhetorical *yes-no* questions:

(1)   Q. Don't you want to grow up big and strong?
       (A. Yes, of course I do.)
(2)   Q. Do you want people to think we live in a pigsty?
       (A. No, of course I don't.)

These examples illustrate a broad and simple generalization that governs the relation between a *yes-no* rhetorical question and the expected answer: "negative rhetorical questions expect positive answers and positive rhetorical questions expect negative answers" (Pope (1976, 37)). This is by no means true of regular *yes-no* questions. These may be neutral as to the expected positivity or negativity of the answer, as in Q. *Can you stand on your head?*, or the expected positivity or negativity of the answer may match that of the question, as in Q. *Has it already started?*, where the expected answer is positive (Pope (1976, 37 f.); the examples Pope's). (On how these ordinary questions may be made rhetorical, see Pope (1976, 38).)

There are several rhetorical questions of the *yes-no* variety in Jackson's speech. They tend to be positive in form, expecting negative answers, as predicted by the rule. For instance, consider the questions in (3a-d):

(3)   a. Can any gentleman affirm to me one proposition that is a
       certain and absolute amendment?
       b. But, in this state, will the prudent merchant attempt alterations?
       c. Will he employ workmen to tear off the planking and take
       asunder the frame?
       d. Are we going to finish in an hour?

All of (3a-d) invite the answer *No.*

In Vining's speech there are again several rhetorical questions of the *yes-no* type, and they complement Jackson's in that they are mostly negative in form. Here are some of them:

(4)	a. ... yet may it not take a considerable proportion of our time?
	b. May it not be procrastinated into days, weeks, nay months?
	c. ... are not vessels daily arriving, and the revenue slipping through our fingers?
	d. Is it not very strange that we neglect the completion of the revenue system?

The answers to all of these rhetorical questions are expected to be positive, in accordance with the rule given.

Turning to *wh* rhetorical questions, we may consider the following questions and expected answers to them, from Pope (1976, 43):

(5)	Q. Who wants yesterday's paper?
	(A. Nobody.)
(6)	Q. Where are we going to get another 1949 Chevy muffler at 11:00 on Sunday?
	(A. Nowhere.)
(7)	Q. Why should we fight Communism?
	A1. No reason, obviously.
	A2. Because it is the greatest evil imaginable, obviously.
(8)	Q. Why should anybody fight Communism?
	A1. There is no reason for anybody to fight Communism.
	A2. *(Anybody should fight Communism) because it is the greatest evil imaginable.

Such examples, especially those in (7), show that the syntax of a *wh* rhetorical question does not always tell us what kind of an answer is expected. The alternatives are generally either "a negative NP — a null set" or "an obvious specific positive answer" (Pope (1976, 42)), and either A1 or A2 could be expected answers to question (7). As far as (5) and (6) are concerned, the answers cited are of the former type, but it is perhaps not impossible to imagine an expected answer of the latter type even in these if the context is set up right. As for (8), however, the negative polarity item *any-* sets up the expectation that the answer is of the negative (null set) type. In the absence of such linguistic clues as negative polarity items, *wh* dependent questions depend on their context of utterance for their expected interpretation. The context includes knowledge and assumptions shared by speaker and hearer, including their knowledge of (and assumptions about) what went before in the discourse. Such knowledge also includes "knowledge of the constraints on the use of sentences" and "of the constraints on conversation or, more generally, on social interaction" (Hudson (1975, 4)). There may be a burden put on the context as far as a *wh* rhetorical question is concerned, more so than in the case of a *yes-no* rhetorical question. Even so, it is still true that for a *wh* rhetorical question to succeed, the expected answer should be clear to both speaker and hearer.

There are several *wh* rhetorical questions in Jackson's speech:

(9)   a. What experience have we had of the good and bad qualities of this Constitution?
b. Then why should we fear a power which cannot be improperly exercised?
c. ... what will be the consequence of taking up this subject?

The expected answers to (9a-b) are clearly negative: "None" and "For no reason," respectively. They fit in well with Pope's observations. As for example (9c), the expected answer is not the negative "None." However, in this case there does not seem to be "an obvious specific positive answer" either, as would be predicted by Pope's account. Rather, the expected answer is something like "The consequence of taking up this subject will be something unmanageable or uncontrollable." Here it seems advisable to extend Pope's account slightly, to allow for positive answers that are not particularly specific.

There are several *wh* rhetorical questions in Vining's speech:

(10)   a. And what object is to be attained by going into a committee?
b. ... how far is it proper to take the subject of amendments into consideration, without the consent of two-thirds of both Houses?
c. What have Congress done towards completing the business of their appointment?
d. And here let me ask gentlemen how they propose to amend that part of the Constitution which embraces the judicial branch of the Government, when they do not know the regulations proposed by the Senate, who are forming a bill on this subject?
e. Suppose every gentleman who desires alterations to be made in the Constitution were to submit his propositions to a Committee

of the Whole; what would be the consequence?

Of these (10e) is reminiscent of Jackson's question listed as (9c). Again the answer is not a negative "Nothing" but positive along the lines of "The consequence will be something unmanageable or uncontrollable." Or, as Vining himself, answering his own rhetorical question, puts it "We should have strings of them contradictory to each other, and be necessarily engaged in a discussion that would consume too much of our precious time."

As for the first four of Vining's *wh* rhetorical questions, they may all be taken to expect negative answers. Answers such as "No object whatsoever," "Not at all proper," "Not nearly enough," and "There is no way," respectively, suggest themselves. The precise form of the answer is not very important. What is important is whether the answer is to be positive or negative. Overall, in both Jackson's and Vining's speeches the answers to *wh* rhetorical questions are overwhelmingly of the latter variety.

The grammatical analysis of *yes-no* and *wh* rhetorical questions demonstrates how the form of a rhetorical question, especially in the case of *yes-no* rhetorical questions, constrains the form of the expected answer, limiting the choices available to the hearer. To explain from a communicative rather than a simply grammatical point of view why this should be the case, we should also investigate Jackson's and Vining's rhetorical questions as speech acts. Regular questions provide a suitable point of departure, if only by way of highlighting their differences from rhetorical questions. Characteristics of regular questions are expressed in John Searle's account on the basis of the four categories of propositional content, preparatory, sincerity and essential conditions:[1]

Propositional content	Any proposition or propositional function.
Preparatory	1. S does not know 'the answer', i.e., does not know if the proposition is true, or, in the case of the propositional function, does not know the information needed to complete the proposition truly (but see comment below).
	2. It is not obvious to both S and H that H will provide the information

	at that time without being asked.
Sincerity	S wants this information.
Essential	Counts as an attempt to elicit this information from H.
Comment:	There are two kinds of questions, (a) real questions, (b) exam questions. In real questions S wants to know (find out) the answer; in exam questions, S wants to know if H knows.

Searle's conditions, while useful for bringing to the fore properties of regular questions, do not fit rhetorical questions. It seems possible to leave the propositional content condition as it stands, but the other conditions must be changed radically. To start with, the rhetorical question "is one to which S is better placed to know the answer than H" (Allan (1986, 223)). Building on this, the following may be proposed as a tentative formulation of the preparatory, sincerity and essential conditions of rhetorical questions (cf. also Allan (1986, 223)):

Preparatory	S is better placed to know the answer to the question than H.
Sincerity	S wants to know whether or not H is willing to concur with or to counter the expected answer to the question.
Essential	Counts as an attempt by S to make H believe that S believes the expected answer and as an attempt by S to make H concur with or counter the expected answer.

This description admits of refinement. In particular, a more sophisticated version might be formulated using the notion of "reflexive-intention." (On this concept, see Allan (1986, 175 f.).) However, even in the present form the analysis brings out the crucial speech act property of a rhetorical question, namely, that rhetorical questions are challenges issued by the speaker to the hearer. The speaker challenges the hearer to accept (concur with) or to reject (counter) the expected answer to the rhetorical question. It is important to add that the options are not on a par. There is a strong expectation for the hearer to concur with rather than to reject the expected answer, to the extent that one might perhaps even restrict the essential condition to this form: "counts as an attempt by S to make H believe that S believes the expected answer and as an attempt by S to make H concur with the expected answer."

The expectation is based on at least two factors. First, in interactional discourse there is a general tendency for a hearer to be cooperative with the speaker. As Allan puts it: "Since it is co-operative to go along with one's interlocutor, H will tend to maintain S's positive face by not disputing a rhetorical question ..., even if he is given the chance" (Allan (1986, 223)).[2] A second factor relates to the nature of the expected answer. The speaker typically phrases his or her rhetorical question in such a way that the expected answer is the only reasonable and logical one possible, given the terms of the question. For instance, we might recall (3a), one of Jackson's rhetorical questions cited above, "Can any gentleman affirm to me one proposition that is a certain and absolute amendment?" Given the difficulty of phrasing and drafting amendments and given the multitude of different proposals for amendments, Jackson must have been confident that no "absolute" amendment could have been forthcoming and that a negative answer was the only reasonable one to his question. Or we might observe the presupposition buried in the relative clause of (9b), another one of Jackson's rhetorical questions, "Then why should we fear a power which cannot be improperly exercised?" The reasonableness of the expected answer ensures that potential opposition, which would have surfaced in the form of an unexpected answer, would be represented as ridiculous or incoherent.

The challenge to the hearer inherent in a rhetorical question constitutes a threat to his or her freedom of action, or to what in politeness theory is called negative face. (On the notion of face, see note 2.) Rhetorical questions have, in fact, been considered a strategy for performing face-threatening acts in the literature. More precisely, Brown and Levinson suggest that they are an "off-record," not an "on-record" strategy.[3] However, the present discussion emphasizes the extent to which the expected answer to a rhetorical question may be recognizable in the context of the utterance in question. This finding gives weight to Brown and Levinson's statement that "many of the classic off-record strategies ... are very often actually on record when used, because the clues to their interpretation (the mutual knowledge of S and H in the context; the intonational, prosodic and kinesic clues to speaker's attitude; the clues derived from conversational sequencing) add up to only one really viable interpretation in the context" (Brown and Levinson (1987, 212)).

The present investigation bears this out in the case of rhetorical questions: even though not all types of clue can be expected to be present in a written text, it is still true that in each of the cases above the expected answer and, as a consequence, the speaker's communicative intention are clear enough. They are so clear that in a sense Jackson's and Vining's rhetorical questions may be regarded as forceful assertions, with expected answers providing the key parts of the assertions. For instance, consider "What have Congress done towards the business of their appointment?" This question and the expected answer, "Not nearly enough," might be expressed as a straightforward declarative: "Congress have not done nearly enough towards the business of their appointment." However, the plain declarative sounds much less forceful.

It should also be emphasized that even though expected answers to Jackson's and Vining's rhetorical questions are obvious and intended to be obvious by the speaker in question, rhetorical questions nevertheless remain questions in grammatical form. This means that they may be answered. More to the point here, they may be answered by the speaker himself. There are several instances of this in the two Congressmen's speeches, especially in Congressman Jackson's speech. For instance, he asks "But, in this state, will the prudent merchant attempt alterations? Will he employ workmen to tear off the planking and take asunder the frame?"; and immediately answers his own rhetorical question "He certainly will not." By answering some of their rhetorical questions themselves, the two Congressmen drive home intended meanings that are obvious anyway. In a sense the device of the rhetorical question with an obvious answer combined with the speaker answering his own question, stating the obvious answer, enables an orator to state his message twice without being accused of repetition. This reinforces the effect that far from being an off-record strategy, the use of rhetorical questions by the two Congressmen is actually an on-record strategy and, it may be felt, a rather presumptive one at that.

Viewing rhetorical questions as challenges presented by the speaker to the hearer, or hearers, as in this case, serves to explain their use in persuasive discourse. It also ties the use of rhetorical questions by Jackson and Vining with their use of imperatives. The speech act force of their imperatives is to direct the hearers (and also the speaker) to do something. In much the same way, the speech act force of their rhetorical questions is to try to make their hearers accept the expected answers to such questions.

While there are no doubt other features of Jackson's and Vining's speeches, including the colorful nautical imagery of Jackson's speech, that merit attention, it has been shown that imperatives and, in particular, rhetorical questions add up to a forceful on-record strategy in their first speeches. As far as their second speeches are concerned, Vining's contains one rhetorical question, but the speech is so short — less than a column in Gales (1834) — that it is hardly possible to base any far-reaching conclusions on it. Jackson's second speech is much longer. Here is a sample, with paraphrases of intended meanings of the first four rhetorical questions added in brackets:

> Let me ask gentlemen, what reason there is for the suspicions which are to be removed by this measure? ['surely there is no reason for ...'] ... Is there a single right that, if infringed, will not affect us and our connexions as much as any other person? ['surely there is not a single right that ...'] Do we not return at the expiration of two years into private life and is this not a security against encroachments? ['surely we return ... and surely this is a security ...'] Are we not sent here to guard those rights which might be endangered, if the Government was an aristocracy or a despotism? View for a moment the situation of Rhode Island, and say whether the people's rights are more safe under State Legislatures than under a Government of limited powers. Their liberty is changed to licentiousness. But do gentlemen suppose bills of rights necessary to secure liberty? If they do, let them look at New York, New Jersey, Virginia, South Carolina, and Georgia. Those states have no bills of rights, and is the liberty of the citizens less safe in those States than in the other of the United States? I believe it is not. (Gales (1834, 442))

The speech is much in the same vein as Jackson's first in that imperatives and rhetorical questions make up a forceful on-record strategy of persuasion in it. As in his first speech, his rhetorical questions allow only one interpretation in their contexts. They are again presumptive and even coercive. And in order to drive home the interpretation in question aggressively, even though it is obvious anyway, Jackson again proceeds to answer some of his rhetorical questions himself.

In the context of the present analysis it comes as no surprise that Jackson won fame in the first Congress because of his loud voice.

Fisher Ames, a fellow member of the first House of Representatives, compared his speaking voice to a "furnace-bellows" and wrote in a letter that Jackson's voice was so loud that the Senate shut their windows "to keep out the din" (Foster (1960, 71)). The window-shutting incident may have occurred in a different debate, but it is not difficult to visualize Congressman Jackson bellowing out his rhetorical questions and then his answers to them in the debate of June 8, 1789.

Madison's Rhetorical Style

The presumptive rhetorical style of Jackson's two speeches and Vining's first speech affords a point of departure for investigating Madison's rhetorical style in the same debate. Both Madison for his part and Congressmen Jackson and Vining for theirs were seeking to persuade their audience, but their means were not the same. As far as rhetorical questions are concerned, the difference is startling, for there is scarcely a single rhetorical question in any of Madison's speeches on that day. Further, there are hardly any *let* imperatives in his speeches either, accentuating the difference in rhetorical posture.

A closer look at the beginning of Madison's central speech sheds light on what his rhetorical style consisted of on that day. For this purpose politeness theory again comes in useful. The very first sentence "I am sorry to be accessary ..." is a straightforward apology (cf. Brown and Levinson (1987, 189)). A little later he observes that he is "compelled to beg a patient hearing ..." These words illustrate another kind of apology: he is saying that he is undertaking a task that impinges on his audience only with reluctance. Apologizing, whether by way of asking for forgiveness or of indicating reluctance, is a strategy for mitigating the threat to the hearer's negative face that may be inherent in a speech act. Another strategy for attenuating threat to negative face that Madison makes frequent use of comes under the label of "Question, hedge" in Brown and Levinson's taxonomy. Strategies of hedging, in particular, are relevant to Madison's speech, for he frequently softens his statements by inserting phrases such as "I think" or "I thought," as at the beginning of the second paragraph. These are "quality hedges" suggesting "that the speaker is not taking full responsibility for the truth of his utterance" (Brown and Levinson (1987, 164)). Some of Madison's *if* clauses likewise serve the function of hedging their respective main clauses, as in "... that is to say, if all power is subject to abuse, that then it is possible the abuse of the powers of the General Government may be guarded against in a more secure manner ..." (On *if* clauses in politeness theory, cf. Brown and Levinson (1987, 162 f.).) Further, there are examples of the strategy "Be conventionally indirect" (Brown and Levinson (1987, 132)) for performing face-threatening acts in Madison's speech. For instance, his suggestion early on that a certain course of action is "desirable" amounts to a request for the course of action to be adopted, but the request is indirect and therefore softened.

The above does not exhaust Madison's strategies. For instance, his willingness to give reasons is worth remarking on. ("Give (or ask for) reasons" is Brown and Levinson's (1987, 128 f.) strategy 13 of positive politeness.) It should also be pointed out that Congressmen Jackson's and Vining's speeches are wholly devoid of the strategies of politeness that have been illustrated in Madison's speech. However, the overall abundance of rhetorical questions in the speeches of the two opponents predominates over such strategies of politeness. Considered as wholes, Jackson's speeches and Vining's first speech are characterized by rhetorical questions and imperatives, while Madison's speech is characterized by such strategies of negative politeness as apologizing, hedging, and conventional indirectness. The former cluster of means of persuasion come across as more presumptive, more coercive, more high-faluting, more in the nature of "speechifying" than the latter. The latter cluster of means, it is suggested here, are not only more low-key but also more sensitive to hearers' face needs. This conclusion presupposes and depends upon the grammatical and speech act analysis of rhetorical questions offered above, which demonstrates that expected answers to rhetorical questions can be recognized, at least as far as Congressmen Jackson's and Vining's speeches are concerned, and that their use of rhetorical questions is not an off-record strategy. (A truly off-record strategy could scarcely be either coercive or presumptive.) In the event, the coerciveness and presumption of their rhetorical questions — bellowed out in Jackson's case, it may be assumed — is reinforced by their answering some of them themselves, thus pre-empting the responses of the audience. By contrast, Madison's speaking voice has been characterized as "weak" (Ketcham ([1971] 1990, 56)), and his strategies of apologizing, hedging, and conventional indirectness do not pre-empt the responses of the audience but pay attention to its face wants, especially as far as negative face is concerned.

Conclusion

It was argued in earlier chapters that the fate of what was to become the Bill of Rights hung in the balance in the United States House of Representatives on June 8, 1789. It is suggested in this chapter that its future — and the future of freedom of information in the United States and elsewhere in later centuries — was impacted by contrasting strategies of persuasion in evidence on that day. No doubt there were other factors that played a role in the debate, including Madison's personal stature and his political background. Even so, one may wonder whether the appeal of Madison's speech might not have lost in effectiveness — and the Bill of Rights might not have been doomed — if it had abounded in imperatives and rhetorical questions, often with ready supplied answers; that is, if Madison had adopted a coercive strategy similar to that of his key opponents. At any rate, Madison's low-key appeal for change worked better than Jackson's and Vining's presumptive strategy for the status quo in the circumstances of this particular debate by the members of the Unites States House of Representatives, those self-selecting immigrants and their descendants.

To say that Madison did not need to resort to a rhetorically presumptive strategy as a vehicle of verbal attack because he had substance on his side is hardly the point, being based on hindsight. To say that he selected his low-key strategy because of his emotional or political self-confidence and maturity — or because of his belief in the maturity of his select audience — may be right but only serves to privilege the role of rhetorical strategies in the debate and the difference in them identified here. Going beyond the concerns of this one debate, the present inquiry raises the question of whether the use of imperatives and rhetorical questions amounts to a presumptive strategy in other political debates and, further, whether a low-key appeal for change is likely to prevail over a more coercive strategy for the status quo more generally, in other circumstances and in front of other audiences, including less select ones. Such issues invite further investigation.

Notes to Chapter 4

1. The analysis is from Searle (1969, 66), with italics omitted from the symbols "S," standing for "Speaker," and "H," standing for "Hearer."

2. Regarding the notion of face and its two aspects, it may be worth quoting a few lines from Brown and Levinson's pioneering work on politeness:

> ... all competent adult members of a society [footnote omitted, JR] have (and know each other to have) ... 'face', the public self-image that every member wants to claim for himself, consisting in two related aspects:
> (a) negative face: [footnote omitted] the basic claim to territories, personal preserves, rights to non-distraction — i.e. to freedom of action and freedom from imposition
> (b) positive face: the positive consistent self-image or 'personality' (crucially including the desire that this self-image be appreciated and approved of) claimed by interactants ... (Brown and Levinson (1987, 61))

3. These concepts are defined by Brown and Levinson as follows:

> An actor goes **on record** in doing an act A if it is clear to participants what communicative intention led the actor to do A (i.e., there is just one unambiguously attributable intention with which witnesses would concur). For instance, if I say 'I (hereby) promise to come tomorrow' and if participants would concur that, in saying that, I did unambiguously express the intention of committing myself to that future act, then in our terminology I went 'on record' as promising to do so.
>
> In contrast, if an actor goes **off record** in doing A, then there is more than one unambiguously attributable intention so that the actor cannot be held to have committed himself to one particular intent. So, for instance, if I say 'Damn, I'm out of cash, I forgot to go to the bank today', I may be intending to get you to lend me some cash, but I cannot be held to have committed myself to that intent ... (Brown and Levinson (1987, 68-

69); their emphasis)

Appendix

Texts of Key Speeches

The text of Mr. Jackson's and Mr. Vining's first speeches and of the beginning of Mr. Madison's third speech, from Gales (1834), with spelling, punctuation, etc. left intact:

Mr. Jackson. — I am of opinion we ought not to be in a hurry with respect to altering the Constitution. For my part, I have no idea of speculating in this serious manner on theory. If I agree to alterations in the mode of administering this Government, I shall like to stand on the sure ground of experience, and not be treading air. What experience have we had of the good or bad qualities of this Constitution? Can any gentleman affirm to me one proposition that is a certain and absolute amendment? I deny that he can. Our Constitution, sir, is like a vessel just launched, and lying at the wharf; she is untried, you can hardly discover any one of her properties. It is not known how she will answer her helm, or lay her course; whether she will bear with safety the precious freight to be deposited in her hold. But, in this state, will the prudent merchant attempt alterations? Will he employ workmen to tear off the planking and take asunder the frame? He certainly will not. Let us, gentlemen, fit our vessel, set up her masts, and expand her sails, and be guided by the experiment in our alterations. If she sails upon an uneven keel, let us right her by adding weight where it is wanting. In this way, we may remedy her defects to the satisfaction of all concerned; but if we proceed now to make alterations, we may deface a beauty, or deform a well proportioned piece of workmanship. In short, Mr. Speaker, I am not for amendments at this time; but if gentlemen should think it a subject deserving of attention, they will surely not neglect the more important business which is now unfinished before them. Without we pass the collection bill we can get no revenue, and without revenue the wheels of Government cannot move. I am against taking up the subject at present, and shall therefore be totally against the amendments, if the Government is not organized, that I may see whether it is grievous or not.

When the propriety of making amendments shall be obvious from experience, I trust there will be virtue enough in my country to make them. Much has been said by the opponents to this Constitution, respecting the insecurity of jury trials, that great bulwark of personal safety. All their objections may be done away, by proper regulations on this point, and I do not fear but such regulations will take place. The bill is now before the Senate, and a proper attention is shown to this business. Indeed, I cannot conceive how it could be opposed; I think an almost omnipotent Emperor would not be hardy enough to set himself against it. Then why should we fear a power which cannot be improperly exercised?

We have proceeded to make some regulations under the Constitution; but have met with no inaccuracy, unless it may be said that the clause respecting vessels bound to or from one State be obliged to enter, clear, or pay duties in another, is somewhat obscure; yet that is not sufficient, I trust, in any gentleman's opinion to induce an amendment. But let me ask what will be the consequence of taking up this subject? Are we going to finish it in an hour? I believe not; it will take us more than a day, a week, a month—it will take a year to complete it! And will it be doing our duty to our country, to neglect or delay putting the Government in motion, when every thing depends upon its being speedily done?

Let the Constitution have a fair trial; let it be examined by experience, discover by that test what its errors are, and then talk of amending; but to attempt it now is doing it at a risk, which is certainly imprudent. I have the honor of coming from a State that ratified the Constitution by the unanimous vote of a numerous convention: the people of Georgia have manifested their attachment to it, by adopting a State Constitution framed upon the same plan as this. But although they are thus satisfied, I shall not be against such amendments as will gratify the inhabitants of other States, provided they are judged of by experience and not merely on theory. For this reason, I wish the consideration of the subject postponed until the 1st of March, 1790. (Gales (1834, 425 f.))

Mr. Vining. — I hope the House will not go into a Committee of the Whole. It strikes me that the great amendment which the Government wants is expedition in the despatch of business. The wheels of the national machine cannot turn, until the impost and collection bill are perfected; these are the desiderata which the public mind is anxiously expecting. It is well known, that all we have hitherto done amounts to nothing, if we leave the business in its present state. True; but, say gentlemen, let us go into committee; it will take but a short time; yet may it not take a considerable proportion of our time? May it not be procrastinated into days, weeks, nay, months? It is not the most facile subject that can come before the Legislature of the Union. Gentlemen's opinions do not run in a parallel on this topic; it may take up more time to unite or concentre them than is now imagined. And what object is to be attained by going into a committee? If information is what we seek after, cannot that be obtained by the gentleman's laying his propositions on the table; they can be read, or they can be printed. But I have two other reasons for opposing this motion; the first is the uncertainty with which we must decide on questions of amendment, founded merely on speculative theory; the second is a previous question, how far it is proper to take the subject of amendments into consideration, without the consent of two-thirds of both Houses? I will submit it to gentlemen, whether the words of the Constitution, "the Congress, whenever two-thirds of both Houses shall deem it necessary, shall propose amendments," do not bear my construction, that it is as requisite for two-thirds to sanction the expediency of going into the measure at present, as it will be to determine the necessity of amending at all. I take it that the fifth article admits of this construction, and think that two-thirds of the Senate and House of Representatives must concur in the expediency as to the time and manner of amendments, before we can proceed to the consideration of the amendments themselves. For my part, I do not see the expediency of proposing amendments. I think, sir, the most likely way to quiet the perturbation of the public mind, will be to pass salutary laws; to give permanency and stability to Constitutional regulations, founded on principles of equity and adjusted by wisdom. Although hitherto we have done nothing to tranquillize that agitation which the adoption of the Constitution threw some people into, yet the storm has abated and a calm succeeds. The people are not afraid of leaving the question of amendments to the discussion of their representatives; but is this the juncture for discussing it? What have Congress done towards completing the business of their appointment? They have passed a law regulating certain oaths; they have passed the impost bill; but are not vessels daily arriving, and the revenue slipping through our fingers? Is it not very strange that we neglect the completion of the revenue system? Is the system of jurisprudence unnecessary? And here let me ask gentlemen how they propose to amend that part of the Constitution which embraces the judicial branch of the Government, when they do not know the regulations proposed by the Senate, who are forming a bill on this subject?

If the honorable mover of the question before the House does not think he discharges his duty without bringing his propositions forward, let him take the mode I have mentioned, by which there will be little loss of time. He knows, as well as any gentleman, the importance of completing the business on your table, and that it is best to finish one subject before the introduction of another. He will not, therefore, persist in a motion which tends to distract our minds, and incapacitate us from making a proper decision on any subject. Suppose every gentleman who desires alterations to be made in the Constitution were to submit his propositions to a Committee of the Whole; what would be the consequence? We should have strings of them contradictory to each other, and be necessarily engaged in a discussion that would consume too much of our precious time.

Though the State I represent had the honor of taking the lead in the adoption of this Constitution, and did it by a unanimous vote; and although I have the strongest predilection for the present form of Government, yet I am open to information, and willing to be convinced of its imperfections. If this be done, I shall cheerfully assist in correcting them. But I cannot think this a proper time to enter upon the subject, because more important business is suspended; and, for want of experience we are as likely to do injury by our prescriptions as good. I wish to see every proposition which comes from that worthy gentleman on the science of Government; but I think it can be presented better by staying where we are, than by going into committee, and therefore shall vote against his motion. (Gales (1834, 429 ff.))

Mr. Madison. — I am sorry to be accessary to the loss of a single moment of time by the House. If I had been indulged in my motion, and we had gone into a Committee of the Whole, I think we might have rose and resumed the consideration of other business before this time; that is, so far as it depended upon what I proposed to bring forward. As that mode seems not to give satisfaction, I will withdraw the motion, and move you, sir, that a select committee be appointed to consider and report such amendments as are proper for Congress to propose to the Legislatures of the several States, conformably to the fifth article of the Constitution.

I will state my reasons why I think it proper to propose amendments, and state the amendments themselves, so far as I think they ought to be proposed. If I thought I could fulfil the duty which I owe to myself and my constituents, to let the subject pass over in silence, I most certainly should not trespass upon the indulgence of this House. But I cannot do this, and am therefore compelled to beg a patient hearing to what I have to lay before you. And I do most sincerely believe, that if Congress will devote but one day to this subject, so far as to satisfy the public that we do not disregard their wishes, it will have a salutary influence on the public councils, and prepare the way for a favorable reception of our future measures. It appears to me that this House is bound by every motive of prudence, not to let the first session pass over without proposing to the State Legislatures some things to be incorporated into the Constitution, that will render it as acceptable to the whole people of the United States, as it has been found acceptable to a majority of them. I wish, among other reasons why something should be done, that those who had been friendly to the adoption of this Constitution may have the opportunity of proving to those who were opposed to it that they were as sincerely devoted to liberty and a Republican Government, as those who charged them with wishing the adoption of this Constitution in order to lay the foundation of an aristocracy or despotism. It will be a desirable thing to extinguish from the bosom of every member of the community, any apprehensions that there are those among his countrymen who wish to deprive them of the liberty for which they valiantly fought and honorably bled. And if there are amendments desired of such a nature as will not injure the Constitution, and they can be ingrafted so as to give satisfaction to the doubting part of our fellow-citizens, the friends of the Federal Government will evince that spirit of deference and concession for which they have hitherto been distinguished.

It cannot be a secret to the gentlemen in this House, that, notwithstanding the ratification of this system of Government by eleven of the thirteen United States, in some cases unanimously, in others by large majorities; yet still there is a great number of our constituents who are dissatisfied with it; among whom are many respectable for their talents and patriotism, and respectable for the jealousy they have for their liberty, which, though mistaken in its object, is laudable in its motive. There is a great body of the people falling under this description, who at present feel much inclined to join their support to the cause of Federalism, if they were satisfied on this one point. We ought not to disregard their inclination, but, on principles of amity and moderation, conform to their wishes, and expressly declare the great rights of mankind secured under this Constitution. The acquiescence which our fellow-citizens show under the Government, calls upon us for a like return of moderation. But perhaps there is a stronger motive than this for our going into a consideration of the subject. It is to provide those securities for liberty which are required by a part of the community; I allude in a particular manner to those two States that have not thought fit to throw themselves into the bosom of the Confederacy. It is a desirable thing, on our part as well as theirs, that a re-union should take place as soon as possible. I have no doubt, if we proceed to take those steps which would be prudent and requisite at this juncture, that in a short time we should see that disposition prevailing in those States which have not come in, that we have seen prevailing in those States which have embraced the Constitution.

But I will candidly acknowledge, that, over and above all these considerations, I do conceive that the Constitution may be amended; that is to say, if all power is subject to abuse, that then it is possible the abuse of the powers of the General Government may be guarded against in a more secure manner than is now done, while no one advantage arising from the exercise of that power shall be damaged or endangered by it. We have in this way something to gain, and, if we proceed with caution, nothing to lose. And in this case it is necessary to proceed with caution; for while we feel all these inducements to go into a revisal of the Constitution, we must feel for the Constitution itself, and make that revisal a moderate one. I should be unwilling to see a door opened for a reconsideration of the whole structure of the Government—for a reconsideration of the principles and the substance of the powers given; because I doubt, if such a door were opened, we should be very likely to stop at that point which would be safe to the Government itself. But I do wish to see a door opened to consider, so far as to incorporate those provisions for the security of rights, against which I believe no serious objection has been made by any class of our constituents: such as would be likely to meet with the concurrence of two-thirds of both Houses, and the approbation of three-fourths of the State Legislatures. I will not propose a single alteration which I do not wish to see take place, as intrinsically proper in itself, or proper because it is wished for by a respectable number of my fellow-citizens; and therefore I shall not propose a single alteration but is likely to meet the concurrence required by the Constitution. There have been objections of various kinds made against the Constitution. Some were levelled against its structure because the President was without a council; because the Senate, which is a legislative body, had judicial powers in trials on impeachments; and because the powers of that body were compounded in other respects, in a manner that did not correspond with a particular theory; because it grants more power than is supposed to be necessary for every good purpose, and controls the ordinary powers of the State Governments. I know some respectable characters who opposed this Government on these grounds; but I believe that the great mass of the people who opposed it, disliked it because it did not contain effectual provisions against the encroachments on particular rights, and those safeguards which they have been long accustomed to have interposed between them and the magistrate who exercises the sovereign power; nor ought we to consider them safe, while a great number of our fellow-citizens think these securities necessary.

It is a fortunate thing that the objection to the Government has been made on the ground I stated; because it will be practicable, on that ground, to obviate the objection, so far as to satisfy the public mind that their liberties will be perpetual, and this without endangering any part of the Constitution, which is considered as essential to the existence of the Government by those who promoted its adoption.

The amendments which have occurred to me, proper to be

recommended by Congress to the State Legislatures, are these: ... (Gales (1834, 431 ff.))

What Happened Later

The later stages of Madison's propositions cannot be followed here in detail, but it deserves to be noted that after June 8, 1789 the question of principle — whether to proceed to consider Madison's amendments or to postpone their discussion by several months or indefinitely — did not come up again at such length or in such an intensive fashion, at least not in the House of Representatives. The following month, on July 21, the House returned to the subject of amendments (Gales (1834, 660-665)). At this meeting the negative options of not committing the propositions to a committee at all or of delaying consideration of them till the spring of 1790 or indefinitely were not seriously proposed. There did ensue a discussion of whether a Committee of the Whole was the best way of proceeding or whether a select committee would after all be more advantageous. A select committee was then instituted and Madison was chosen as one of its members (Gales (1834, 665)).

The select committee worked fast, and reported to the House as early as July 28. The report was taken up on August 13, after a brief last-minute effort initiated by Thomas Sedgwick to postpone the matter had been voted down (Gales (1834, 704-707)). (In the debate James Jackson was silent and even John Vining now advocated early consideration of amendments, see Gales (1834, 704-707).)

In the following days the House of Representatives proceeded to devote a considerable amount of time to discussing amendments. One issue that provoked a great deal of debate was the question of whether the amendments should be incorporated into existing articles of the Constitution or whether they should stand together as a separate part of the Constitution. Madison, for one, favored the former option, but Roger Sherman insistently advocated the latter. The former option prevailed in a vote on August 13, but on August 19 the House reversed the decision (Gales (1834, 707, 766)). With hindsight, it is easy to see how the decision to have the amendments as a separate part was an extraordinarily happy one, for in this form the Bill of Rights has come to be looked upon as a well-defined and cohesive symbol of individual rights and liberties. That this course of action was advocated by Roger

Sherman, who had been among the Representatives most hostile to amendments, including in the debate of June 8, is almost paradoxical.

Apart from the form of attachment, a great deal of time was of course also devoted in the House of Representatives to considering specific formulations of individual amendments. The key provisions for the freedom of speech and of assembly came up on August 15. Here Thomas Sedgwick moved to delete the provision for the right to assemble but received very little support, with those speaking against Sedgwick's motion including Representatives Gerry, Page, and even Vining (Gales (1834, 731-733). More generally, the consideration of amendments had at this point taken on such a momentum that the House was able to submit its proposals for amendments to the Senate in late August (Rutland (1983, 209)).

In the Senate, which met in secret, there was a move to delay consideration of the amendments, but it was defeated (cf. Bowling (1990, 143)). In September 1789 the Senate then moved speedily to consider the amendments proposed, reducing their number to twelve. In the process "the Senate rejected that amendment which Madison said he prized above all the others, the one that prohibited the states from infringing on personal rights" (Rutland (1983, 212); cf. also Bowling (1990, 144)). On September 19, the Senate reformulations of the amendments were back in the House. A conference committee was appointed, consisting of three House members, Madison being one, and of three Senate members, and by September 25 both Houses had reached agreement on the precise wording of each amendment (Rutland (1983, 214 f.)).

Comparing the final wording of the ten amendments with what Madison proposed in his third speech on June 8, 1789, one cannot but be impressed by the similarity that they bear to Madison's original submission. For instance, we might sample the crucial first amendment as a case in point. Here is Madison's proposal:

> Fourthly. That in article 1st, section 9, between clauses 3 and 4, be inserted these clauses, to wit: The civil rights of none shall be abridged on account of religious belief or worship, nor shall any national religion be established, nor shall the full and equal rights of conscience be in any manner, or on any pretext, infringed.
>
> The people shall not be deprived or abridged of their right to speak, to write, or to publish their sentiments; and the freedom of the press, as one of the great bulwarks of liberty, shall be inviolable.
>
> The people shall not be restrained from peaceably assembling and

consulting for their common good; nor from applying to the Legislature by petitions or remonstrances, for redress of their grievances. (Gales (1834, 434))

And here is article I of the Federal Bill of Rights, as promulgated on December 15, 1791:

> Congress shall make no law respecting an establishment of religion, or prohibiting the free exercise thereof; or abridging the freedom of speech, or of the press; or the right peaceably to assemble, and to petition the Government for a redress of grievance. (Rutland (1983, 243))

With both Houses having approved the amendments, they were forwarded to the President, to be submitted to the States. State ratifications followed fairly speedily, with New Jersey and Maryland leading the way, but it took over two years to reach the requisite number. (Two minor amendments, one on apportioning seats in the House of Representatives and the other on congressional salaries, failed to achieve ratification, cf. Rutland (1983, 216 f.).) The requisite number of States was reached on December 15, 1791, when Virginia, Madison's home State, became the eleventh to ratify the ten amendments (Rutland (1983, 217)). The momentum generated by Madison on June 8, 1789 had carried the process to its conclusion.

Chapter 5

Process and Activity in *To Autumn*

To Autumn

1

Season of mists and mellow fruitfulness,
  Close bosom-friend of the maturing sun;
Conspiring with him how to load and bless
  With fruit the vines that round the thatch-eves run;
To bend with apples the moss'd cottage-trees,
  And fill all fruit with ripeness to the core;
    To swell the gourd, and plump the hazel shells
  With a sweet kernel; to set budding more,
And still more, later flowers for the bees,
Until they think warm days will never cease,
    For summer has o'er-brimm'd their clammy cells.

2

Who hath not seen thee oft amid thy store?
  Sometimes whoever seeks abroad may find
Thee sitting careless on a granary floor,
  Thy hair soft-lifted by the winnowing wind;

Or on a half-reap'd furrow sound asleep,
  Drows'd with the fume of poppies, while thy hook
  Spares the next swath and all its twined flowers:
And sometimes like a gleaner thou dost keep
  Steady thy laden head across a brook;
  Or by a cyder-press, with patient look,
  Thou watchest the last oozings hours by hours.

3

Where are the songs of spring? Ay, where are they?
  Think not of them, thou hast thy music too,—
While barred clouds bloom the soft-dying day,
  And touch the stubble-plains with rosy hue;
Then in a wailful choir the small gnats mourn
  Among the river sallows, borne aloft
  Or sinking as the light wind lives or dies;
And full-grown lambs loud bleat from hilly bourn;
  Hedge-crickets sing; and now with treble soft
  The red-breast whistles from a garden-croft;
  And gathering swallows twitter in the skies.[1]

John Middleton Murry once remarked of this ode: "It is the perfect and unforced utterance of the truth contained in the magic words: 'Ripeness is all'" (Murry ([1925] 1964, 189)). And F. R. Leavis responded: "Such talk is extravagant, and does not further the appreciation of Keats. No one could have found that order of significance in the Ode merely by inspecting the Ode itself" (Leavis ([1936] 1949, 263)).

"Inspecting the ode itself" invokes an important methodological principle. It is in keeping with Leavis's more general view of Keats: "The current placing of him seems, in essentials, likely to stand: what a critic may still propose to himself is a sharper explicitness; a recall, that is, to strict literary criticism" (Leavis ([1935] 1949, 241)).

The following pages seek to be strict and explicit about the ode, which has been called Keats's "most perfect" (Ward (1963, 321)), "for many readers the finest" (Allot (1976, 39)), or "markedly the greatest of Keats's odes" (Ricks ([1974] 1984, 208)). For the most part the present reading will rely solely on "the ode itself," and on the indisputably relevant contemporary letter from Keats to J. R. Reynolds.

Up to a point, the interpretation suggested here entails calling into question some parts of the recent and characteristically eloquent interpretation of the poem provided by Helen Vendler. More positively, the methodological point of view adopted, focussing on intrinsic evidence, will make it possible to identify two hitherto neglected patterns of grammatical recurrence in the poem. The poetic function of the linguistic patterns discovered here will be addressed at the end of this contribution.

The methodological perspective adopted here supports a more literal and a less "mythic" reading of the poem than has been the case in a number of relatively recent studies. Among those arguing for mythic implications of the poem is that by S. R. Swaminathan (1981). However, it is with refreshing and comforting candor that he states that "the poem does not explicitly refer to any myths ... " (Swaminathan (1981, 392)). In this respect the poem differs from some others by Keats, but this difference may only have contributed to its enduring appeal, especially these days when interest in, and knowledge of, mythology has been on the decline.

The first stanza opens with two noun phrases. Autumn is (the) "season of mists and mellow fruitfulness" and (a) "close bosom-friend of the maturing sun." Autumn conspires with the sun to do many things, expressed by a series of verb phrases: "load and bless / With fruit the vines," "bend with apples the moss'd cottage-trees," "fill all fruit with ripeness to the core," "swell the gourd," and "plump the hazel shells / With a sweet kernel." As Freeman (1978, 5 f.) points out, at the phrase structure level these verb phrases have almost identical structures, of the pattern Verb — Noun Phrase — Prepositional Phrase, and they exhibit a high degree of syntactic parallelism.

From a semantic point of view, the stanza is dominated by the related notions of maturing and mellowness. To mature is to become mature or to cause to become mature. The ambiguity is inherent in *the maturing sun,* as has been observed by Freeman (1978, 9 f.). The stanza is dominated thematically by adjectives and verb constructions which are more or less closely linked in meaning: *mellow, load with fruit, fill with ripeness, swell, plump with a kernel.* In addition to syntactic parallelism, there is thus a pattern of semantic recurrence in the stanza. (On the notion of linguistic recurrence as a sign of poetic form, see Kiparsky (1973, 233 f., 243).)

The adjective *soft* is less closely connected with the idea of maturing but is related to it in a broader sense, especially by way of the adjective *mellow*. (It is instructive to consider the different senses of the adjective *mellow* in the OED. In several of them, *soft* or a derivative of *soft* appears.) It occurs once in the second stanza and twice in the third, contributing to the thematic content and coherence of the poem as a whole.

In the first stanza autumn is anthropomorphized. In the second it is more clearly personified. However, the poem stops short of saying whether the figure of autumn is male or female. In order not to have to refer to the figure by the pronoun *it*, which seems inappropriate for a personified figure, a female figure will be assumed here. Possible sources of inspiration for the second stanza, as discussed by Jack (1967, 232 ff.) and Davenport (1959, 97), tend to support the view that the figure is female.[2] However, such considerations are necessarily extrinsic to the poem and cannot therefore be decisive.

The second stanza details four spatial locations where the personified figure of autumn may be found: "sitting careless on a granary floor," "on a half-reap'd furrow," soundly asleep while her "hook / Spares the next swath," carrying a load on her head across a brook and watching "the last oozings" of a cyder-press.

The third stanza provides a description of the music of autumn. The music, located temporally first by *while* and *then* and later by *now,* is of different kinds: "the small gnats mourn" "in a wailful choir," "full-grown lambs ... bleat," "hedge-crickets sing," "the red-breast whistles" in a soft treble, and "gathering swallows twitter." The stubble plains constitute the spatial location for this music, but the sounds issue from different places: the bleating of lambs from a hilly bourn, the whistling of a red-breast from a garden-croft and the twittering of swallows from the skies.

The setting of the ode points to the central image of the stubble plains. To quote Vendler: "The whole poem, to my mind, is uttered from the stubble-plains ... " (Vendler (1983, 255)). Vendler's statement is perhaps something of a hyperbole, for it is difficult to maintain that the first and second stanzas are uttered from the stubble plains. If this quibble is set aside, it is possible to agree with her that the image is crucial in the third stanza and important in the whole poem. However, Vendler's interpretation of the symbolic value of this central image is in some ways difficult to accept. She suggests that the stubble plains imply deprivation, arguing that the tones of the poem, "even of greatest celebration, are, I think, intelligible only when they are heard as notes issuing from deprivation." On the next page, she speaks of "the obdurate blankness of the stubble-plains from which the spirit of the corn has fled." Three pages later she goes on to argue that — following the departure of what she likewise takes to be the female figure — the scene is one of desolation, like "the desolation of the little town robbed by the urn of its inhabitants ..." (Vendler (1983, 259)). She claims further that "by his deliberate invoking of gnats (small and wailful and helpless in the wind, however light), and by his infantilizing of sheep (as bleating lambs), as well as by his attributing a 'treble soft' to the red-breast, Keats suggests that the post-sacrificial autumn music issues from a choir of orphans" (Vendler (1983, 259)). She goes on to suggest that in the poem Keats is recalling a Shakespearean sonnet, "using its constellation of orphans and diminished birdsong."[3]

It is hardly possible to prove that Keats was thinking of a Shakespearean sonnet when composing his ode. By the same token, it is equally difficult to prove that Keats was not thinking of a Shakespearean sonnet. When writing *To Autumn,* he was no doubt in some sense aware of his earlier ode *On a Grecian Urn.* However, the value of Vendler's comparison of the two odes may be questioned, in the absence of a more direct parallel of the image of the stubble field in the earlier ode. At best her references to a Shakespearean sonnet and to the other ode constitute circumstantial and indirect evidence for interpreting the later ode.

More direct evidence regarding the image of the stubble plains is of two kinds; Keats's letter to J. R. Reynolds and the poem itself. The letter stands out from others[4] and has a privileged status, because it contains an actual reference to the inspiration that gave rise to the ode. The poem was composed on September 19, 1819 and the letter is from September 21, 1819. (On this chronology, see Murry ([1925] 1964, 190).)

How beautiful the season is now—How fine the air. A temperate sharpness about it. Really, without joking, chaste weather—Dian skies—I never lik'd stubble fields so much as now—Aye better than the chilly green of the spring. Somehow a stubble plain looks warm—in the same way that some pictures look warm—this struck me so much in my sunday's walk that I composed upon it. (Gittings (1970, 291 f.))

The letter hardly sustains an interpretation founded on melancholy or death (cf. also Jugurtha (1985, 191)). Instead, the comparison with spring that is evoked and the depiction of the stubble plain convey a feeling above all of warmth.

If there were evidence in the poem itself to support Vendler's claim that the stubble fields furnish a scene of desolation, of obdurate blankness, and that the sounds are those of orphans, it might be conceivable to play down or to ignore the significance of the letter to Reynolds, in spite of the fact that it makes specific reference to the poem. However, there is little warrant in the poem for such a view, rather the opposite. The gnats are "small" and they are "borne aloft" or they sink "as the light wind lives or dies." The sound that they make is "wailful" and, as Walter J. Bate puts it, the reader "is free to associate the wailful mourning of the gnats with a funeral dirge for the dying year ..." (Bate (1963, 583)). The association links up with the image of the wind which "lives or dies," suggesting, in Mayhead's words, "the particular position of autumn, poised between the brilliant 'life' of summer and the 'death' of winter" (Mayhead (1967, 100 f.)). The association may be made, but it should be relativized in a number of ways. First, it is worth recalling the associations of autumn for Keats. It is traditional to associate autumn with "death, decay, and ravishment," but such associations are by no means characteristic of Keats, as Jugurtha (1985, 111 f., 191) has demonstrated. She shows convincingly that, on the contrary, Keats linked autumn with "gold, maturity, and fruitfulness" (Jugurtha (1985, 111)). Second, the adjective "wailful" may be taken to be descriptive of the monotony of the sound, and as Bate notes, the sound of gnats "is no more confined to autumn alone than is the 'soft-dying' of any day ..." (Bate (1963, 583)). Indeed, one would more readily associate gnats with summer than with winter. In this context, the reader might justifiably recall Keats's *Ode to a Nightingale,* with its murmurous sound of "flies on summer eves." Third, Vendler's claim that the gnats are "helpless" seems reductive. The gnats, after all, make their sounds in a choir, and, as noted by Nicholas Royle (personal communication) the word "choir" suggests a sense of purpose and of unity — not a sense of helplessness.

As regards the questions at the beginning of the third stanza, these have been taken to express a "sad longing for what was lovely and is gone" (Davenport (1959, 96)). However, any feeling of sad longing is immediately overcome and transcended by the confident imperative *Think not of them, thou hast thy music too.*

As for the context of the music:

While barred clouds bloom the soft-dying day,
And touch the stubble-plains with rosy hue;
Then ...

The day is dying, but softly, "without pain" (Ricks ([1974] 1984, 210)), and "bloomed" by the clouds. The choice of *bloom* seems significant (cf. also Hartman (1973, 310)). The verb means 'to give a bloom to', 'to colour with a soft warm tint or glow' (OED, under sense 5 of the verb). It evokes a visual image, also recalling the flowers of the first stanza and linking up with *rosy hue* in the next line. The noun phrase *barred clouds* is the subject of both *bloom* and *touch,* and the blooming and the touching are simultaneous and fused as part of the same process. This fusion heightens concentration and intenseness, inviting deepened reader involvement in the scene. The synaesthesia of *touch ... with rosy hue,* pointed out by Nicholas Royle (personal communication), similarly serves to intensify sensory perceptions. It is certainly difficult to see blankness or desolation in these lines. On the contrary, we have a picture of the clouds imbuing the soft-dying day with a roseate warmth and beauty, in a manner reminiscent of the description in Keats's letter to J. R. Reynolds.

Keats's poem is hardly about desolation and deprivation, let alone about orphans. It is rather about the season of autumn, celebrating its natural warmth, beauty, mellowness and maturity. Recalling the anthropomorphized and personified figure of autumn, the poem may be seen as a celebration not only of the season of autumn but also of the age of maturity in the life of a human being.

And there is something more. The present reading of the poem is further illuminated by features of language that have gone largely unnoticed in earlier scholarship. It has been noted that the "constitutive trope of the ode *To Autumn* is enumeration, the trope of plenitude" (Vendler (1983, 266); cf. also Macksey (1984, 298, 302)). In the same context the large number of verbs in the poem has been remarked upon. However, what has not been sufficiently appreciated is that more important than any sheer number of verbs is their quality. More specifically, it is helpful here to refer to an important linguistic distinction which was first developed systematically by George Lakoff in the 1960's and has since become commonplace in linguistic theory, viz., the division of verbs into dynamic and stative. This distinction rests on several differences, but the one which has stood the test of time best is probably the admissibility of the progressive *-ing* form:

dynamic verbs typically allow it while stative verbs typically do not.[5] What is striking in the ode, then, is the overwhelming prevalence of dynamic verbs. There are some stative verbs in the poem, such as *run*, in its relevant sense here, and *think* in the first stanza, *see* in the second stanza, and *be* (twice), *have*, and *live* in the third stanza, but their number is very small. Virtually all of the remaining verbs in the ode, which number approximately forty, are dynamic. For instance, *twitter*, *whistle*, *sing*, and *bleat*, taken in reverse order from the third stanza, all easily allow the progressive, as in *They are twittering, whistling*, etc. *Think*, in the second line of the third stanza, is interesting, for this verb is generally stative (cf. *I think that* ... versus ?*I am thinking that* ...). However, the imperative construction, as in the poem, brings out a dynamic interpretation of the verb, for it will be recalled that the admissibility of imperatives is actually one of the other original criteria satisfied by dynamic verbs (Lakoff (1966, 1)).

Underpinning the grammatical division of verbs into dynamic and stative there is of course a semantic difference. Stative verbs denote qualities and states, and dynamic verbs denote processes, acts, activities, accomplishments and events. (For a discussion of semantic classes of verbs in this context, see Quirk et al. (1985, 200 ff.).) The prevalence of dynamic verbs gives the poem a dynamic quality, highlighting the processes, acts, activities, accomplishments and events that take place in the poem.

However, simply to assert that there is a dynamic quality to the poem, on the basis of the frequency of dynamic verbs, would be reductive, and not true to the spirit of the poem. We should be sensitive to a second grammatical pattern in the poem, one that is intimately linked to the first, but has the effect of moderating it. To appreciate this second pattern, it is worth considering a line whose force has sometimes been neglected by earlier commentators: *Until they think warm days will never cease.* This line has sometimes been taken to be a mere prosaic comment on the erroneousness of the bees' belief. The belief may be factually erroneous, but that is hardly the point of the line in the poem. Nor does such prosaism do justice to the spirit of a Romantic poem. What the line does is emphasize the sense of duration and of non-completion, so that the moment, the day, and the season become "never-ceasing." It seems significant that the day is never completed in the poem. In the third stanza the day is dying, but it is not dead. It is from this perspective of non-completion, or of "never-ceasing," that a second pattern of recurrence emerges: there are significant instances of present participles or progressive -*ing* forms spread over the poem. They begin with *maturing,* and include *conspiring, budding, winnowing,* and *gathering.* The progressive -*ing* form typically expresses processes, acts, and activities that are taking place but are unfinished. Such is the case with the progressive -*ing* forms in the poem.

Nor is the use of the progressive the only means by which the effect of "never-ceasing" is accomplished. In the second stanza a number of activities are "stationed" or suspended (cf. Bate (1963, 582) and Macksey (1984, 296)). The effect of non-completion that is denoted by suspension is underlined by such adverbials of manner or of time as *patiently* and *hours by hours.* Also, the actions of the figure of autumn are iterative, as is clear from the repetition of *sometimes* in the stanza. Iterated actions are in progress in a broader sense, because they are repeated an unspecified number of times. Past participles, in general, do express completion, but here even this property is repeatedly moderated, by forms such as *soft-lifted* and *half-reaped.* Such modified past participles highlight the manner, or indeed even the lack of the completion of the action, rather than its fulfillment or result.

In the third stanza, the verbs *bloom, touch, mourn,* etc. are in the simple present tense, but much the same effect of action in progress is achieved by the thematically linked temporal expressions *while* (that happens), *then* (this happens), and *now* (this happens). In the third stanza we also encounter the poet's choice of *gathering* over *gather'd.* (On these variants, cf. Ridley (1933, 288) and Stillinger (1974, 258 f.).) This choice is striking, but also entirely natural in the context of the present interpretation.[6]

The ode is about the season of autumn, and, in a transferred sense, about the age of maturity in the life of a human being. The present interpretation privileges the large number of processes, acts and events that take place at this season. Dying is recognized in the poem as one of these, but the poem does not contemplate autumn and the age of maturity primarily as seasons of desolation or of blankness when processes, actions and events are completed, finished and then dead. Rather, the poem is lighter and warmer. It celebrates autumn and the age of maturity as seasons when a very large number of processes and actions are in progress: some of them languorously suspended, others more intense. Overall, such variety of "never-ceasing" process and activity denotes richness, not death and desolation.

Notes to Chapter 5

1. The text of the poem is from Stillinger's (1978, 476 f.) edition. The author also takes this opportunity to record his indebtedness to Adrienne Lehrer and Gerald McNiece, of the University of Arizona, and Nicholas Royle, of the University of Tampere, who read and provided valuable comments on an earlier version of the present chapter. There is no doubt that the chapter would have been improved if more of their suggestions had been incorporated into the chapter.

2. Cf. Jack (1967, 232 ff.) and Davenport (1959, 97). The question of whether the figure might be that of Ruth, as argued for by Davenport (1959, 99) and, earlier, by Gwynn (1952, 472 f.), or whether the figure might be that of Psyche, as argued for by Swaminathan (1981, 394 f.), is set aside here, since the present analysis is primarily focused on explicit properties of the poem and neither of these figures is explicitly mentioned in the poem.

3. The sonnet in question is sonnet 97.

4. Such other letters include the one to Richard Woodhouse, from September 21, 22, which contains a copy of the poem (Gittings (1970, 294 f.)). On the special features of this letter copy, and, more broadly, on extant holographs of the poem, see Stillinger (1974, 258 f.); for a reproduction of the first draft of the poem, see Finney ([1936] (1963, 706 f.).

5. See Lakoff (1966). For instance, to support the progressive *-ing* criterion, Lakoff contrasts *I am learning that* with **I am knowing that*. For later discussion and development of the stative versus dynamic distinction, see Sag (1973).

6. Here it seems worth glancing at Macksey's (1984) fairly recent interpretation of the poem, because the choice of *gathering* over *gather'd* seems important as regards the persuasiveness of the interpretation. He recognizes the sense of plenitude in the poem, and especially in the third stanza, but proceeds to introduce emptiness and absence: "the poem projects no further after the season of harvest, only death and the nothingness of absence," arguing that a calm acceptance of death and absence "makes possible one's authentic existence" (Macksey (1984, 306)). He supports his ideas of death and absence by setting up a progression of sensory perceptions from the kinaesthetic, in the first stage, through the visual or observational, in the second stage, to the auditory, in the final stage (Macksey (1984, 294, 302)) and by arguing that only when "the reader's relation to the scene is most attenuated" (in the final stage) are we "most vividly aware of its innumerable activities and transitory life" (Macksey (1984, 302)). Further, he suggests that the swallows of the final

line "have been reaped in their moment of plenitude, that the absoluteness of their being is defined for man ... by the fact of their immanent nonbeing" (Macksey (1984, 306 f.)). He then concludes that "by recognizing his emptiness as potential receptivity instead of struggling to overcome it, ... Keats succeeded at the end in creating a poem that marks the crossing from the poetry and poetics of Romanticism" (Macksey (1984, 307)).

Macksey's reading is subtle and eloquently phrased, but the present author finds difficulty in accepting its premises and therefore hesitates to consider "death and the nothingness of absence" as keys to interpreting the poem. First, Macksey's view of a progression of sensory perceptions should be relativized, in view of the emphasis on locational phrases in the final stanza. These phrases evoke the visual sense, as the one normally associated with identifying locations. More pointedly, the synaesthesia of *touch ... with rosy hue* undercuts the idea of attenuation in the third stanza. The effect that the synaesthesia achieves is the very opposite, one of intensification of sensory perceptions and of heightened involvement on the part of the poet and the reader. This effect of intensification carries over to and embraces the auditory perceptions that follow, given the close temporal link that is established by means of *while ... then*. Second, there is the poet's choice of *gathering* over *gather'd* in the final line: the choice of the present participle over the past participle undercuts the view of seeing the swallows as "reaped." Yet to maintain his interpretation Macksey is forced to use the past participle even when phrasing it. For such reasons, the present author still prefers to emphasize the sense of plenitude and activity in progress in the poem, rather than "death and the nothingness of absence."

Chapter 6

Pleading with an Unreasonable King: the Kent and Pauline Episodes in Shakespeare

The Kent episode in *King Lear* and the Pauline episode in *The Winter's Tale* have not often, if ever, been considered in conjunction, but this chapter will suggest that to fail to do so is to miss important similarities in the structure and conception of the two episodes.[1] The former is about 70 lines in length, running from the second half of line 119 to line 186 of I.i.; from this the approximately ten lines of Lear's first speech addressed to Cordelia can be set aside, as can Kent's farewells at the end.[2] The latter episode is slightly longer, some 90 lines and, runs from the second half of line 39 to line 129 of II.iii. (Pauline's interaction with a lord and a servant in the lines just prior to these can be set aside.) Here are the texts of the episodes, according to the Arden editions:

Kent.   Good my Liege,—
Lear. Peace, Kent!
    Come not between the Dragon and his wrath.
    I lov'd her most, and thought to set my rest
    On her kind nursery. ...
Kent.   Royal Lear,
    Whom I have ever honour'd as my King,
    Lov'd as my father, as my master follow'd,

As my great patron thought on in my prayers,—
Lear. The bow is bent and drawn; make from the shaft.
Kent. Let it fall rather, though the fork invade
The region of my heart: be Kent unmannerly,
When Lear is mad. What would'st thou do, old man?
Think'st thou that duty shall have dread to speak
When power to flattery bows? To plainness
    honour's bound
When majesty falls to folly. Reserve thy state;
And, in thy best consideration, check
This hideous rashness: answer my life my judgment,
Thy youngest daughter does not love thee least;
Nor are those empty-hearted whose low sounds
Reverb no hollowness.
Lear.   Kent, on thy life, no more.
Kent. My life I never held but as a pawn
To wage against thine enemies; nor fear to lose it,
Thy safety being motive.
Lear.   Out of my sight!
Kent. See better, Lear; and let me still remain
The true blank of thine eye.
Lear. Now, by Apollo,—
Kent.   Now, by Apollo, King,
Thou swear'st thy Gods in vain.
Lear.   O, vassal! miscreant!
                    [*Laying his hand upon his sword.*
Alb., Corn. Dear Sir, forbear.
Kent. Kill thy physician, and the fee bestow
Upon the foul disease. Revoke thy gift;
Or, whilst I can vent clamour from my throat,
I'll tell thee thou dost evil.
Lear.   Hear me, recreant!
On thine allegiance, hear me!
That thou hast sought to make us break our vow,
Which we durst never yet, and with strain'd pride
To come betwixt our sentence and our power,
Which nor our nature nor our place can bear,
Our potency made good, take thy reward.
Five days we do allot thee for provision
To shield thee from disasters of the world;
And on the sixth to turn thy hated back
Upon our kingdom: if on the tenth day following
Thy banish'd trunk be found in our dominions,
The moment is thy death. Away! By Jupiter,

This shall not be revok'd.

Kent. Fare thee well, King; ...

        (I.i.119-123; 138-179) (Muir ([1952] 1972, 11-15))

Leon.   What noise there, ho?

Paul. No noise, my lord; but needful conference

    About some gossips for your highness.

Leon.   How!

    Away with that audacious lady! Antigonus,

    I charg'd thee that she should not come about me.

    I knew she would.

Ant.   I told her so, my lord,

    On your displeasure's peril and on mine,

    She should not visit you.

Leon.   What! canst not rule her?

Paul. From all dishonesty he can: in this—

    Unless he take the course that you have done,

    Commit me for committing honour—trust it,

    He shall not rule me.

Ant.   La you now, you hear:

    When she will take the rein I let her run;

    But she'll not stumble.

Paul.   Good my liege, I come,—

    And, I beseech you hear me, who professes

    Myself your loyal servant, your physician,

    Your most obedient counsellor, yet that dares

    Less appear so, in comforting your evils,

    Than such as most seem yours;—I say, I come

    From your good queen.

Leon.   Good queen!

Paul. Good queen, my lord, good queen: I say good queen,

    And would by combat make her good, so were I

    A man, the worst about you.

Leon.   Force her hence.

Paul. Let him that makes but trifles of his eyes

    First hand me: on mine own accord I'll off;

    But first, I'll do my errand. The good queen

    (For she is good) hath brought you forth a daughter;

    Here 'tis; [*Laying down the child*] commends it to your

        blessing.

Leon.   Out!

    A mankind witch! Hence with her, out o'door:

    A most intelligencing bawd!

Paul.   Not so:
I am as ignorant in that, as you
In so entitling me: and no less honest
Than you are mad; which is enough, I'll warrant,
As this world goes, to pass for honest.
Leon.   Traitors!
Will you not push her out? Give her the bastard,
Thou dotard! thou are woman-tir'd, unroosted
By thy dame Partlet here. Take up the bastard,
Take't up, I say; give't to thy crone.
Paul.   For ever
Unvenerable be thy hands, if thou
Tak'st up the princess, by that forced baseness
Which he has put upon 't!
Leon.   He dreads his wife.
Paul. So would I you did; then 'twere past all doubt
You'd call your children yours.
Leon.   A nest of traitors!
Ant. I am none, by this good light.
Paul.   Nor I; nor any
But one that's here, and that's himself; for he,
The sacred honour of himself, his queen's,
His hopeful son's, his babe's, betrays to slander,
Whose sting is sharper than the sword's; and will not
(For, as the case now stands, it is a curse
He cannot be compell'd to 't) once remove
The root of his opinion, which is rotten
As ever oak or stone was sound.
Leon.   A callat
Of boundless tongue, who late hath beat her husband,
And now baits me! This brat is none of mine;
It is the issue of Polixenes.
Hence with it, and together with the dam
Commit them to the fire!
Paul.   It is yours;
And, might we lay th' old proverb to your charge,
So like you, 'tis the worse. Behold, my lords,
Although the print be little, the whole matter
And copy of the father: eye, nose, lip;
The trick of's frown; his forehead; nay, the valley,
The pretty dimples of his chin and cheek; his smiles;
The very mould and frame of hand, nail, finger:
And thou, good goddess Nature, which hast made it
So like to him that got it, if thou hast

The ordering of the mind too, 'mongst all colours
No yellow in 't, lest she suspect, as he does,
Her children not her husband's!
Leon.   A gross hag!
And, lozel, thou art worthy to be hang'd,
That wilt not stay her tongue.
Ant.   Hang all the husbands
That cannot do that feat, you'll leave yourself
Hardly one subject.
Leon.   Once more, take her hence.
Paul. A most unworthy and unnatural lord
Can do no more.
Leon.   I'll ha' thee burnt.
Paul.   I care not:
It is an heretic that makes the fire,
Not she which burns in 't. I'll not call you tyrant;
But this most cruel usage of your queen—
Not able to produce more accusation
Than your own weak-hing'd fancy—something savours
Of tyranny, and will ignoble make you,
Yea, scandalous to the world.
Leon.   On your allegiance,
Out of the chamber with her! Were I a tyrant,
Where were her life? she durst not call me so,
If she did know me one. Away with her!
Paul. I pray you do not push me; I'll be gone.
Look to your babe, my lord: 'tis yours: Jove send her
A better guiding spirit! What needs these hands?
You, that are thus so tender o'er his follies,
Will never do him good, not one of you.
So, so: farewell; we are gone.   *Exit.*
       (II.iii.39-129) (Pafford ([1963] 1968, 45-50))

In both episodes there is a protracted appeal to a king from a person of lower rank who pleads not for himself or herself but rather for a third party. The third parties, Cordelia in one case and the Queen and the baby girl in the other, are persons closely linked to the king by family ties. Furthermore, in both scenes the pleading encounters reluctance and resistance on the part of the king. Such similarities between the two episodes are important, but it will be suggested in this chapter that there are additional affinities that are revealed by methods of linguistic pragmatics. Two such methods will be applied in the following. These are the methods of conversation analysis and of speech act analysis. The methods are linked and cannot be sharply separated, but they nevertheless arise from different research traditions, and applying first one and then the other will help to structure the present discussion. No systematic review can be given here of the history of either research tradition and the discussion must be limited to what is of immediate significance for the investigation of the two episodes. Admittedly, both research traditions of linguistic pragmatics were originally conceived for the study of "natural" (unscripted) conversation, not of drama, and there are differences between the two types of discourse, some of which, for instance, have to do with the presence of a projected audience in the case of drama.[3] Principles devised for the analysis of "natural" conversation cannot therefore be blindly applied in the study of drama. However, it is at the same time clear that the two types of discourse are intimately connected and there is by now something approaching a consensus in the literature that in general methods of linguistic pragmatics can be applied to the study of drama, including Shakespearean dialogue, even if at times some modification or fine-tuning of such methods may be necessary.[4]

Conversation analysts have observed that conversations exhibit a number of features of a general nature. The following may be quoted from Sacks et al. (1974, 700 f.; references to subsections omitted), as especially relating to turns and to turn-taking:

(1) Speaker-change recurs, or at least occurs.
(2) Overwhelmingly, one party talks at a time.
(3) Occurrences of more than one speaker at a time are common, but brief.
(4) Transitions (from one turn to a next) with no gap and no overlap are common. Together with transitions characterized by slight gap or slight overlap, they make up the vast majority of transitions.
(5) Turn order is not fixed, but varies.
(6) Turn size is not fixed, but varies.
(7) Length of conversation is not specified in advance.
(8) What parties say is not specified in advance.
(9) Relative distribution of turns is not specified in advance.
(10) Number of parties can vary.
(11) Talk can be continuous or discontinuous.
(12) Turn-allocation techniques are obviously used. A current speaker may select a next speaker (as when he addresses a question to another party); or parties may self-select in starting to talk.
(13) Various 'turn-constructional units' are employed; e.g., turns can be projectedly 'one word long', or they can be sentential in length.

(14) Repair mechanisms exist for dealing with turn-taking errors and violations; e.g., if two parties find themselves talking at the same time, one of them will stop prematurely, thus repairing the trouble.

This list of features of conversation should be supplemented with the notion of topic and of topical coherence. The term "topic" may be defined as "what the text (or part of the text) is about" (Allan (1986, 110)). (On the question of how to represent topics, see Rudanko (1993a, 43 ff.).) As for topic coherence, it "is something *constructed* across turns by the collaboration of participants" (Levinson (1983, 315); Levinson's emphasis). It is often signalled by devices of cohesion (coreferring noun phrases and pro-forms, lexical cohesion, etc.), although these do not in themselves necessarily guarantee a shared topic (cf. Halliday and Hasan (1976, 31 ff. and 274 ff.), van Dijk (1981, 186 f.), and Levinson (1983, 314 f.)). However topics are signalled, the notion has unquestionable psychological reality to participants in a conversation, for in the unmarked case they relate their contributions to the topic at hand and failure to do so is liable to be noticed and may become an item for comment. Further, if participants wish to change the topic, they use largely conventionalized means of accomplishing it.[5] An example might clarify the point. Near the beginning of II.iii of *Othello* Iago and Cassio have a conversation whose topic is Desdemona until Iago engineers a topic change (cf. also Rudanko (1993a, 38 f.)):

> *Iago.* ... our general cast us thus early for the love of his Des-
> demona, who let us not therefore blame: he hath not
> yet made wanton the night with her; and she is sport
> for Jove.
> *Cas.* She is a most exquisite lady.
> *Iago.* And I'll warrant her full of game.
> *Cas.* Indeed she is a most fresh and delicate creature.
> *Iago.* What an eye she has! methinks it sounds a parley of
> provocation.
> *Cas.* An inviting eye, and yet methinks right modest.
> *Iago.* And when she speaks, 'tis an alarm to love.
> *Cas.* It is indeed perfection.
> *Iago.* Well, happiness to their sheets! . . . Come, lieuten-
> ant, I have a stoup of wine, and here without are a
> brace of Cyprus gallants, that would fain have a
> measure to the health of the black Othello.
> (II.iii.14-29) (Ridley ([1958] 1966, 69-70))

Up to Iago's last turn, Desdemona is clearly the mutually constructed topic in the conversation, Iago's and Cassio's turns being tightly linked by such devices of cohesion as coreferring pro-forms, which in this case refer to Desdemona. However, with his last turn Iago engineers a smooth transition to a new topic, that of drinking Othello's health. The transition is signalled in part by the particle *well*, which continues to have a function bearing on topic and topic-shifting in present-day English (cf. Labov and Fanshel (1977, 156), Svartvik (1980, 177), and Schiffrin (1987, 102 ff.)).

Armed with such notions of conversation analysis, we may now return to the speech events from *King Lear* and *The Winter's Tale*.[6] One of the most interesting here of the 14 features of conversation is feature 12, which relates to allocation of turns. For much of the time in the two episodes, the principle "A current speaker may select a next speaker ..." operates in reverse, as it were, along the lines of "A current speaker may block a certain speaker from taking a turn," for Lear and Leontes try to prevent Kent and Pauline, respectively, from taking turns. Both do so repeatedly and in forceful terms. Lear tries to silence Kent for instance with "Peace, Kent!" (120) and "Kent, on thy life, no more" (153). For his part, Leontes tries to stop Pauline from having a turn by repeatedly asking her to leave or by asking others to remove her, either by the force of words or by physical action: "Away with that audacious lady!" (42), "Force her hence" (61), "Out!" (66), "Hence with her, out o' door:" (67), "Will you not push her out?" (73), "Once more, take her hence" (111). At times there are also attempts to select the next speaker in order to exclude another. Thus Leontes turns to others and especially to Antigonus repeatedly, using the speaker-selects-next-speaker technique. However, the technique is apt to fail, as in line 46 "What! canst not rule her?", when Pauline comes in before Antigonus answers the question addressed to him, and similarly around line 77, when Pauline again comes in, pre-empting the turn selected by Leontes for Antigonus.

At a slightly more subtle level there is a noticeable similarity in the way the petitioners, Kent and Pauline, respond to and cope with attempts to silence them. For instance, when Lear says "The bow is bent and drawn; make from the shaft" (142), Kent responds "Let it fall rather, though the fork invade / The region of my heart:" (143-144). That is, Kent, orienting his turn to Lear's by employing cohesive devices (*the shaft — it —* the lexically related *the fork*), is able to build on Lear's words, turning them around to his own use. A similar relation holds between Lear's "Kent, on thy life, no more" (153) and Kent's "My life I never held but as a pawn / To wage against thine enemies; nor fear to lose it, / Thy safety being motive" (154-156) and between Lear's "Out of my sight!" (156) and Kent's "See better, Lear; and let me still remain / The true blank of thine eye" (157-158). Further examples can be cited from the Pauline episode, including Leontes's "What! canst not rule her?" (46), addressed to Antigonus, and Pauline's reply "From all dishonesty he can:" (47). Cohesion of this kind is observed in one or two of Leontes's speeches, but on the whole it is more rare in the two kings' speeches. Cohesion and orienting one's turn to the previous speaker's turn tend to make one's conversational contribution sound reasonable and considered, in that the speaker pays attention to the other party. On the other hand, the lack of cohesion, especially in Lear's speeches, carries the implication of peremptoriness and lack of sensitivity. Such findings have a bearing on the division of audience sympathies in the episodes.

As for other features on Sacks et al.'s list, number 8 is "what parties say is not specified in advance." Here it is observed that the first attempts by both Lear and Leontes to stop Kent and Pauline from speaking take place even before they (or the audience) learn what the latter two want to say. This creates a sense that Lear and Leontes "know," or presume to "know," in advance what Kent and Pauline are going to say, and thus set themselves above feature 8.

Another feature on the list that sheds light on the two interchanges is 14, which relates to turn-taking violations, such as two speakers speaking at the same time. (Repair mechanisms for violations seem less central in the present context, simply because violations are often not repaired.) Interruptions in conversation may be accommodated here. It has been emphasized in work subsequent to Sacks et al. (1974) that these may be of two basic types: supportive and disruptive (cf., for instance, West (1978), (1979), West and Zimmerman (1983), and Tannen (1989)). In a supportive interruption a speaker is interrupted by a second speaker who expresses enthusiasm for what the first speaker is saying, while in a disruptive interruption a speaker is confronted with disagreement or with a challenge for the floor while he or she is speaking. (Often a disruptive interruption involves both disagreement and a challenge for the floor simultaneously.) There is no "norm" for interruptions of either type or for reactions or responses to them, but it is clear that disruptive interruptions, especially those contesting the right to the floor, are dispreferred variants of conversational responses.

Yet it is precisely these types of interruptions that are found especially in the *Lear* extract. At the very beginning of the extract Lear cuts Kent off in mid-sentence, after the address "Good my Liege,—" (119). Kent's second turn is longer "Royal Lear, / Whom I have ever honour'd as my King, / Lov'd as my father, as my master follow'd, / As my great patron thought on in my prayers,—" (138-141), but even here he does not get beyond the terms of address before Lear interrupts him in a disruptive fashion. Kent too engages in a disruptive interruption later on. When Lear says "Now, by Apollo,—" (159) Kent cuts him off in mid-sentence, disruptively, by coming in with "Now, by Apollo, King, / Thou swear'st thy Gods in vain" (159-160) before Lear can complete his sentence. However, by and large disruptive interruptions by the petitioners are much more rare in the episodes.

A first conclusion here is that in the extracts there are deviations of different types from the conventions governing turn-taking in conversation. Such deviations are marked or dispreferred options and their presence explains in part why the exchanges are felt to be confrontational in nature. Further, it may be felt that conversational conventions are not violated in arbitrary ways but rather in ways that on the whole tend to present the petitioners as the more reasonable conversationalists. The petitioners are admittedly turned into challengers in the course of the conversations, but this is presented as mainly resulting from the confrontational hostility of the two kings. The impression of hostility, in turn, results in large part from the exercise of dispreferred conversational options by the kings. A measure of audience sympathy accrues to the underdogs as a consequence.

Looking at the scenes from the point of view of speech act theory, it seems clear that a dominant speech act in the two episodes is the directive. For instance, Lear's turns such as "Kent, on thy life, no more" (153) and "Out of my sight!" (156) are a variety of directives. (In their surface forms neither of these sentences has an expressed verb, but a verb may be understood, along the lines of "Kent, on thy life, say no more!" and "Get out of my sight!") Here is Searle's analysis of the speech act of requesting, based on the four types of conditions, propositional content, preparatory, sincerity and essential, together with comments on ordering and commanding:[7]

Propositional content	Future act A of H.
Preparatory	1. H is able to do A. S believes H is able to do A.

	2. It is not obvious to both S and H that H will do A in the normal course of events of his own accord.
Sincerity	S wants H to do A.
Essential	Counts as an attempt to get H to do A.
Comment	*Order* and *command* have the additional preparatory rule that S must be in a position of authority over H. *Command* probably does not have the 'pragmatic' condition requiring non-obviousness. Furthermore in both, the authority relationship infects the essential condition because the utterance counts as an attempt to get H to do A *in virtue of the authority of S over H*.

The content of directives in the two episodes is overwhelmingly similar. They are requests or orders by Lear and Leontes for the challenger to fall silent or to leave.

Account should also be taken of questions put by Leontes. Questions are often considered a subclass of directives, since to ask a question is to ask the hearer to supply some information. However, questions can also be used as indirect directives to request some action other than the supplying of information (cf. Searle (1975, 65 ff.)). Questions by Leontes often serve this purpose, as in "Will you not push her out?" (73). Being conventionally indirect is often considered a feature of politeness (cf. Brown and Levinson (1987, 132 ff.)), but this is scarcely the case here. Both on account of the negative *not* and on account of the context, especially of what went before in Leontes's speeches ("Force her hence" (61), "Out!" (66), etc.), the directive is peremptory and insistent in tone, demanding compliance from the hearer.

A dominant speech act of the two kings, then, is the directive, performed either directly or indirectly. It might also be expected that a fair number of directives would occur in the speeches of Kent and Pauline, since in both scenes each of them is pleading for someone. There are some directives from them, as in Kent's "Reserve thy state; / And, in thy best consideration, check / This hideous rashness" (148-150) and in Pauline's "Let him that makes but trifles of his eyes / First hand me" (62-63), but overall the number is rather low in comparison with what is found in the two kings' speeches. It should be added that while Pauline's utterance "The good queen / (For she is good) hath brought you forth a daughter— / Here 'tis; [*Laying down the child*] commends it to your blessing" (64-66) is a request for Leontes's acceptance, it is indirect and less insistent than Leontes's questions used as indirect directives. In the two episodes the challengers, even though they are asking for something, come across as more reasonable, on account of the relatively low number of their directive speech acts and on account of the less peremptory nature of their directives.

There is another type of speech act that is very dominant in the speeches of the two kings. Informally, this is the speech act of name-calling, calling one's interlocutor or interlocutors names that are in some way unpleasant or distasteful. In the literature the term "dysphemistic epithets" has been used with reference to many of Coriolanus's speech acts (Rudanko (1993a, 144 f.)), and the same term might be employed here. Dysphemistic epithets might be defined as follows:[8]

Propositional content	Some imputed or projected categorization C of H.
Preparatory	S thinks that C reflects discredit on H and S thinks that H thinks that C reflects discredit on H.
Sincerity	S values C negatively.
Essential	Counts as an expression of contumely or deprecation of H by means of attributing or imputing C to H.
Comments	Epithets in general attribute some categorization to a person or group of people. The opposite of a dysphemistic epithet is a euphemistic — or, perhaps more accurately, a eulogistic — epithet.

The speeches of the two kings abound in dysphemistic epithets. Here are some examples. Lear calls Kent a "miscreant" (160) and a "recreant" (165), while Leontes calls Pauline "a mankind witch" (67), "a most intellingencing bawd" (68), "A callat / Of boundless tongue" (90-91), "A gross hag" (107), and "lozel" (108). Not only does

Leontes hurl his invective and dysphemistic epithets at Pauline, but his attendants, including Antigonus, likewise get their plentiful share of them. Thus Leontes calls them "Traitors" (72), "A nest of traitors" (81), and Antigonus receives the ad hominem dysphemistic epithet of "dotard" (74) into the bargain.

Again, the speeches of the challengers are not entirely devoid of epithets or even dysphemistic, or at least negative, ones. Thus both Kent and Pauline use the word "mad" (Kent 145, Pauline 72) with reference to the king. However, on the whole, the number of their dysphemistic epithets is considerably lower and, as far as the broader class of epithets is concerned, there are also qualitative differences. In particular, their epithets are often not dysphemistic but may in fact be construed as eulogistic or at least as respectful, as in Kent's phrases "my father" (140), "my master" (140), and "my great patron" (141). Further, their epithets do not necessarily refer to the king but rather they may use them to refer to themselves or to a third party not present on the stage. Thus Kent calls himself the king's "physician" (162) and Pauline calls herself the king's "loyal servant" (54), his "physician" (54), and "most obedient counsellor" (55). (The use of the word "physician" is perhaps enough to alert the audience to a connection between the two scenes.) As far as epithets referring to third parties not present on the stage are concerned, the positive "good queen" is introduced by Pauline (58) and in the exchange that follows Shakespeare almost allows her the upper hand. At any rate, the use of the term is contested or questioned by Leontes and emphatically reaffirmed and repeated by Pauline, and as a whole the subepisode about the use of the term further underlines the importance of epithets in the episode. Terms of address are perhaps not epithets *per se*, but the respectful usage of both Kent and Pauline early on in the episodes, usages such as "Royal Lear" (Kent, 138) and "my lord" (Pauline, 40) is also worth observing in the present context.

All in all, dysphemistic epithets are an important and frequently occurring speech act in the speeches of the two kings in the two episodes. The challengers likewise use epithets, but these are more varied, more balanced and less often dysphemistic.

This survey has traced three rhetorical patterns as predominant in the speech behavior of the kings in the two episodes: their resort to disruptive interruptions and other violations of unmarked turn-taking conventions, to imperious directives and to dysphemistic epithets. In Shakespeare criticism, as in other criticism, such findings relating to features of language pose the question of what they mean and how such rhetorical patterns can be linked with psychological ones. To attempt an answer to this question is to undertake an interpretive step and here caution must be exercised. However, the three rhetorical patterns discovered here might be associated with a desire on the part of the kings to try to assert their power over — or even to manipulate — their co-conversationalists. As far as dysphemistic epithets in particular are concerned, they are loaded labels, and the two kings' frequent resort to them may be viewed as an attempt to assert their power not only over their co-conversationalists but over reality itself. This latter effect arises because dysphemistic epithets are designed to change and to distort reality.[9] At another level, the rhetorical patterns favored by the two kings might be traced to a sense of insecurity on their part. They do not feel secure and self-confident enough to face out the petitions and challenges in an orderly way, but have to resort to tactics that are more or less peremptory and disruptive of conversational interaction or are designed to distort reality. It should also be observed how in both scenes third parties on the stage, persons who may be presumed to be loyal subjects of the king, evince sympathy or even outright physical support for the challengers. Thus Albany and Cornwall protect Kent's life, and Leontes's many commands to his attendants to remove Pauline by brute force are spectacularly unsuccessful. For their part, the tactics of disruption, manipulation and reality-distortion on the part of the two kings conspire to bring about a measure of audience sympathy for the pleaders, for the underdogs, in the two scenes.

In the two episodes Shakespeare confronted the question of how to present a challenge to a king from a subject with a just grievance, a delicate problem in the society in which he was writing. In the conversational exchanges in question the kings' speeches contain elements that ensure that a considerable amount of audience sympathy accrues to the underdogs, and there is a remarkable similarity between the scenes in this respect. At the same time, this finding must be immediately moderated and counterbalanced by the consideration that towards the end of each episode the king regains a measure of his self-assurance and perhaps of audience sympathy. Lear does not use his sword and instead pronounces a more deliberate sentence, and at the end of the other episode Shakespeare allows Leontes the exquisite rhetorical question "Were I a tyrant, / Where were her life?" (121-122), which he answers himself "she durst not call me so, / If she did know me one" (122-123). The rhetorical question and the answer to it denote a return of detachment and of self-confidence. There is a measure of sympathy shown for the challenger in both episodes, but at the end of each episode the rhetorical and psychological equilibrium is restored, with the king asserting his authority in a manner that is accepted without argument by those present, including the challengers. The analysis here cannot resolve the question of whether the effect of the episodes in question is to undermine or to underpin royal authority, the former by way of sympathy accruing to the challengers and the latter by way of the hierarchical and rhetorical equilibrium being restored at the end of each episode. What the present article does is to clarify the rhetorical progression of acts and actions in the episodes, highlighting the applicability of methods of linguistic pragmatics to this end.

Notes to Chapter 6

1. The author is grateful to James Hurford, of the University of Edinburgh, for reading and commenting on the next to final version of this chapter at the 1995 LSA Institute in Albuquerque. Of course, the author alone is responsible for remaining shortcomings of the final version.

2. The textual references in this article are to the Arden editions of the plays, with details given after each extract.

3. On the special properties of dramatic discourse, see for instance Downes (1989, 228 f.).

4. Cf., in the present context, Coulthard (1977, 171), Downes (1989, 226 ff.), Herman (1991, 97 ff.), Rudanko (1993a, 18 f.) and Bennison (1993, 79 ff.).

5. On topic change, cf. Covelli and Murray (1980) and Levinson (1983, 314 f.).

6. For another study, conceived independently of the present one, of the application of conversation analysis to the first episode, see Herman (1991, 114 ff.).

7. The analysis is from Searle (1969, 66), preserving the emphasis of the original but elsewhere omitting the italics of the symbols "A," for "Act," "H," for "Hearer," and "S," for "Speaker."

8. The account is from Rudanko (1993a, 144 f.), with slight modifications. The term "eulogistic epithet" was coined by Ian Gurney, personal communication.

9. Here we are reminded of Dubrow's (1987, 28 ff.) account of the effect of naming and misnaming in *Venus and Adonis*.

Coda: Discretionary and Non-Discretionary Acts and Actions in Shakespeare

The purpose of this coda is to suggest that it is useful in the analysis of Shakespearean drama to distinguish two types of acts or actions: one type is made up of those whose outcome or even inclusion is more or less dictated to the playwright by the sources, by the artistic conventions at the time of writing or by the genre, while the other type comprises those over whose inclusion and shaping the playwright seemingly has more discretion. Actions of the first type are also typically necessary to propel the main plot of a play, while those of the second type, so far from propelling it, may actually retard its unfolding. To facilitate discussion, acts and actions of the first type will be termed "non-discretionary," and those of the second type "discretionary."

The feasibility and value of the distinction between discretionary and non-discretionary acts and actions can only be gauged on the basis of concrete examples and illustrations. The illustrations here are from *Coriolanus*, in order to motivate the distinction independently of the two plays examined in the body of the chapter. Towards the end of V.ii of the play Menenius undertakes his mission to save Rome but is rebuffed by Coriolanus in rather short order. Early in the next scene Coriolanus says the following to Aufidius:

> ... Fresh embassies and suits,
> Nor from the state nor private friends, hereafter
> Will I lend ear to. (*Shout within.*) Ha! what shout is
>   this?
> Shall I be tempted to infringe my vow
> In the same time 'tis made? I will not.
>   (V.iii.17-21) (Brockbank (1976, 287))

Immediately after these words of Coriolanus, there comes the entry of Virgilia, Volumnia, young Marcius and attendants. Thereupon

Coriolanus proceeds straightaway to lend an ear to the suit of the party, and after the pleading of Volumnia, to grant the request to save Rome.

Some of the acts or actions of Coriolanus included in this brief sketch group themselves into the two types as follows, arranged in the order in which they occur in the temporal sequence:

Coriolanus swears not to listen to any more suits to save Rome — discretionary

Coriolanus reaffirms his resolve not to listen to any more suits to save Rome — discretionary

Coriolanus listens to, and grants, the suit to save Rome — non-discretionary

The distinction between discretionary and non-discretionary actions no doubt glosses over many complexities of analysis that are inherent in the description of behavior in Shakespearean drama. Everything that happens in a play is part of the plot in a broad sense and the notion of a main plot, which comprises some actions but not others, is hard to define formally and can probably only be grasped intuitively. Views may also differ on what is dictated to the playwright by artistic convention and what is not, and some acts or actions may be in a gray area, neither wholly discretionary nor wholly non-discretionary. Alternatively, the distinction may be conceived of as one of degree in the first place, with acts or actions ranged on a scale, with discretionary and non-discretionary ones being at the opposite ends of a continuum and others falling somewhere in between. Whatever the precise form or format in which the distinction between discretionary and non-discretionary acts may be couched, it seems that the three acts of Coriolanus listed above underpin the distinction in a fairly straightforward fashion. After all, it would scarcely have been imaginable, from an artistic point of view, for Shakespeare to have Coriolanus reject Volumnia's request and burn down Rome. Such an outcome would have strayed too far from his source and from most people's sense of artistic convention (and would have destroyed the main plot of the play) to have been a credible option for Shakespeare. Therefore, this action of Coriolanus is non-discretionary from the playwright's point of view. On the other hand, there is no constructional necessity whatever arising from the main plot or from artistic convention for Shakespeare to have Coriolanus volunteer his promise to Aufidius not to listen to any more suits. The same holds true equally or even more so for his volunteering a reaffirmation of the promise. Volumnia and the others could just as well have entered a few lines earlier, and Coriolanus's promise and the reaffirmation of it only slow down or retard the unfolding of the main plot. To the extent that such judgments can be reciprocated by other readers and spectators it may be felt that the distinction between discretionary and non-discretionary acts and actions has some validity. As far as the present author is aware, the distinction is novel, at least in these terms, both in the voluminous Shakespeare literature and in the literature on stylistics.

Both non-discretionary and discretionary acts and actions are important from a critical point of view and neither can be viewed in isolation. The former are often "big" actions, of the type of Coriolanus saving Rome, which are impossible to ignore. However, the latter, by their very nature, are apt to provide a more nuanced angle on the artist's conception of the character in question. For instance, as far as the discretionary actions adduced above from *Coriolanus* are concerned, they bring out an important feature of the behavior and of the character of the main protagonist of the play. It is a critical truism, based, for instance, on his words to Aufidius "I do hate thee / Worse than a promise-breaker" (I.viii.1-2) (Brockbank (1976, 140)), that he is fond of professing to hate promise-breaking and lack of constancy above everything else. However, the sequence of the discretionary acts of promising and then of reaffirming the promise, followed by the non-discretionary act of breaking the promise shortly after making and then reaffirming it, highlight his own lability and lack of constancy.

A playwright has more or less total freedom of choice over the inclusion and shaping of discretionary acts and actions. It may be held therefore, for instance in the case of the example cited, that such actions, by their very nature, are peculiarly revealing of the artist's conception of his or her characters and of the ways that the audience may perceive them and respond to them.

The Kent and Pauline episodes treated in the main body of this chapter are of the discretionary variety, since they are incidental to the main plot. When they are studied in conjunction, they may therefore be held to provide a window on Shakespeare's conception of the possibilities for representing scenes of confrontation between a king and his subject.

Chapter 7

Case Roles in Literary Translation: an Example from Shakespeare

The purpose of the present chapter is to examine case roles, also called thematic roles or relations, in translation. (The terms "case role" and "thematic role" will here be used interchangeably.) Thematic roles of arguments, expressed in theta theory, constitute a major aspect of the semantic structure of sentences. Therefore, if a target language text is to correspond with its source language counterpart in respect of meaning, the thematic structures of the two should be similar. If the concept of translation equivalence is used, viewed "as a dialectic between the signs and the structures within and surrounding the SL and TL texts" (Bassnett-McGuire ([1980] 1991, 29)), it is possible to suggest that the study of thematic structure offers a handle on the task of explicating one aspect of this notion. The present investigation is focused on determining the extent to which case roles are preserved or changed in translation, as illustrated by one concrete case study. Some comments are also included on the artistic implications of changes of thematic structure.

Case roles of subjects of sentences in two of Othello's soliloquies and in two of Iago's soliloquies are examined in Shakespeare's original play and in two standard translations of the play into Finnish, those by Cajander (1916) and Jylhä (1955). The soliloquies in question are those at III.iii.262 ff. and V.ii.1 ff. for Othello and those at II.i.281 ff. and

II.iii.327 ff. for Iago. In the case of Othello's soliloquy at III.iii.262 ff. full line-by-line analyses are provided of the original and of the two translations, with comments on points of difficulty. To save space, analyses of the remaining soliloquies and of their translations are not produced, but the numerical results are given. (The originals are analyzed in Rudanko (1993a, 90 f., 94 f., 96 f.).)

Soliloquies have been selected for investigation here because of their important function in Shakespearean tragedy. As the critic Una Ellis-Fermor puts it: "... at its finest, as at the height of the Elizabethan period, the soliloquy, by its rapid and profound revelation of thought and passion, serves the very ends of drama. It reveals what we could not otherwise divine of the depths of the speaker's mind, compressing into some twenty lines of vivid illumination what might else have taken the better part of an act to convey" (Ellis-Fermor (1946, 105)).

As regards the focus in this investigation of soliloquies, the study of grammatical subjects does not amount to a full account of thematic relations in sentences. However, as recognized in current syntactic theory, the subject has a privileged status in a sentence, in that it is an obligatory constituent of a sentence (cf., for instance, Chomsky (1986, 4)). This special status of subjects motivates their selection for consideration here.

Even with the limitation of this study to grammatical subjects, there is quite a broad range of case roles to be considered, and these roles should be defined as explicitly as possible at the outset, so that it becomes possible to apply them to an authentic literary text. This task is complicated by the fact that at the present time, there is as yet no one system of thematic relations that has gained universal acceptance among all linguists. For the present study the system of cases to be adopted is that of Rudanko (1993a, 64 ff.). This system is not the most elaborate in the literature, but perhaps partly for that reason it is one that seems suited to the analysis of literary texts.

Here is the list of case roles to be used, with definitions and with an example of each in the subject position:

A, for Agent, "the case of the typically human perceived willful instigator of the action described in the sentence" (Rudanko (1993a, 70)), as in ***John*** *kissed Mary.*

I, for Instrument, "the case of the inanimate force or object causally involved in the action or state identified by the verb" (Fillmore (1968, 24)), as in ***Circumstances*** *reduced John to poverty.*

E, for Experiencer, the case of "the person experiencing sensation, emotion, or cognition" (Cook (1989, 191)), as in *John knows his limitations*.

B, for Benefactive, the case of "the possessor of an object or [of] the nonagentive party in the transfer of property" (Cook (1989, 191)), as in *John received a visitor*.

O, for Object, in Cook's (1989, 191) system the case of "the neutral underlying theme of the state, process, or action described by the verb," but in the present system, the case of "the neutral underlying theme" of a process or action verb, as in *John died unexpectedly*.

Os, for Object$_{stative}$, the case of Object when the verb is stative, as in *John is tall*.

As will be clear, the system outlined is indebted to Walter Cook's (1989) framework in a number of important ways. (It may not be a coincidence that Cook's system has likewise been applied to the analysis of literary texts, cf. Cook (1979, 167-179) and Cook (1989, 209 f.).) For instance, the present system, like Cook's, is non-localist in that it has the Benefactive case role, while lacking the Source and Goal case roles. Further, it is also similar to Cook's system in that it uses coreferential case roles, where the simultaneous assignment of two case roles to a single NP may be felt to characterize the properties of the NP in question more adequately than a single case role. (For examples, see below.) On the other hand, the present system differs from Cook's framework in employing the Instrument case role, along the lines of Charles Fillmore's early work (see Fillmore (1968)), and in distinguishing O and Os as distinct case roles.

The definitions of case roles given above are based on semantic properties of NPs or, more particularly, on the relationships that NPs have with verbs and adjectives. These definitions guide the practical assignment of case roles to sentences. However, sometimes it is also possible to supplement meaning-based definitions with tests that are at least partly syntactic or grammatical in nature. For instance, in the case of Agents, it is often possible to consider the insertion of a manner adverbial such as *carefully*. (For this test, see Gruber (1967).) This kind of manner adverbial is more compatible with agentive than with nonagentive interpretations. For instance, recalling Gruber's pioneering discussion, we may consider the contrast between *John looked through the glass carefully,* where *look* takes an Agent as its subject, and **John saw through the glass carefully,* where *see* selects an Experiencer in the corresponding position. Or we may recall Jackendoff's (1972, 34) sentence *Max rolled down the hill.* This is ambiguous in isolation in that its subject may or may not be an Agent, but the insertion of *carefully,* as in *Max rolled carefully down the hill,* produces a sentence that quite definitely favors an agentive interpretation.

The admissibility of purpose clauses, typically beginning with *in order to,* may be used as another criterion of agentivity, for such clauses are similarly more compatible with agentive than with nonagentive sentences (cf. Gruber (1976, 161) and Rudanko (1993a, 68 f.)). This test confirms the difference between *look* and *see* that was proposed on the basis of the insertability of *carefully,* for *John looked through the glass in order to find out what was going on* seems more readily possible than **John saw through the glass in order to find out what was going on.* And as predicted, in Jackendoff's sentence the insertion of a purpose clause brings out an agentive interpretation, as witness *Max rolled down the hill, in order to attract attention.* (Rolling down the hill may be a quaint way of attracting attention, but this does not affect case assignment.) It may be added that since both tests bring out agentive interpretations, it is also predicted that they are compatible with each other and can be applied simultaneously. This is seen in *John looked through the glass carefully in order to find out what was going on* and in *Max rolled carefully down the hill in order to attract attention,* both of which are well formed.

The two tests are only a sample of tests of agentivity, but they are perhaps sufficient in the present context. (For additional discussion of such tests, cf. Rudanko (1993a, 66 ff.).) Such tests are useful in providing a grammatical grounding for the identification of case roles.

We may now turn to the text of Othello's first soliloquy. The case roles of subjects in it may be analyzed as follows (Rudanko (1993a, 87 ff.)):

Oth. This fellow's of exceeding honesty,	Os
And knows all qualities, with a learned spirit,	E
Of human dealing: if I do prove her haggard,	A; Os
Though that her jesses were my dear heart-strings,	Os
I'ld whistle her off, and let her down the wind,	A; A
To prey at fortune. Haply, for I am black,	A; Os
And have not those soft parts of conversation	B
That chamberers have, or for I am declin'd	B; Os
Into the vale of years,—yet that's not much—	Os
She's gone, I am abus'd, and my relief	A=O; Os; Os
Must be to loathe her: O curse of marriage,	E

That we can call these delicate creatures ours,	A
And not their appetites! I had rather be a toad,	Os
And live upon the vapour in a dungeon,	O
Than keep a corner in a thing I love,	A=B; E
For others' uses: yet 'tis the plague of great ones,	Os
Prerogativ'd are they less than the base,	Os; Os
'Tis destiny, unshunnable, like death:	Os
Even then this forked plague is fated to us,	A/Passive
When we do quicken: Desdemona comes,	O; A=O
If she be false, O, then heaven mocks itself,	Os; A
I'll not believe it.	E

(III.iii.262-283) (Ridley ([1958] 1966, 109 f.))

One caveat of a general nature deserves to be inserted at this point with respect to case role assignments. (For the caveat, see also Rudanko (1993a, 100).) Case role assignment, here as elsewhere in this investigation, is explicit and categorical. Explicitness is no doubt a worthy goal and useful as a heuristic strategy, but at the same time the very categoricality of case roles may at times inevitably lead to decisions that gloss over nuances of thematic meaning. For instance, with respect to Agents, it may be the case that some Agents are more agentive than others in the sense of passing more tests of agentivity or of passing such tests more readily. The use of coreferential case roles, as in the system of case roles employed here, alleviates this problem to some extent but does not entirely remove it. In one or two instances there may also be some hesitation involved in the assignment of case roles. In the final analysis, this caveat in respect of case role assignment is a consequence of the very nature of case roles: these "should be thought of as points delimiting a space where predicates are located" (Rudanko (1989, 59)). Looking at it from the point of view of an individual predicate, it is only to be expected that "not every predicate is equidistant from the point nearest to it" (Rudanko (1989, 59)). It can only be hoped that the judgements made here with respect to case role assignment can be reciprocated to a considerable extent by others who are familiar with the system of case roles used here.

Turning to the task of assigning case roles to subjects in the soliloquy, it may be observed that there are understood subjects of different kinds in the extract. For instance, in "I had rather be a toad, / And live upon the vapour in a dungeon," the subject of *live* has been elided and is easily supplied from the previous sentence. In "let her down the wind, / To prey at fortune," the subject of *prey* has not been elided in the same way, but is rather PRO, an abstract pronominal element with the features of number, case and gender, but without overt lexical or phonetic realization.

As far as dynamic passives are concerned, provision should likewise be made for logical or understood subjects, even though none necessarily appears in the realized sentence in question. A dynamic passive should be seen in opposition to a stative (or statal) passive. The distinction may be explicated with an illustration that is ambiguous, potentially permitting either reading. A sentence such as *The door was closed* is a case in point. This may be paraphrased 'the door was not open', which reading focuses on a state or the result of an action, or it may be paraphrased 'the door was closed by some unspecified entity', which interpretation focuses on the act or action of someone or something closing the door. The former reading is stative, the latter dynamic. (For further discussion of the two types of passive, see Cook (1990, 25 ff.) and Rudanko (1993a, 75 ff.).) In the extract, there are examples of each type: "Even this forked plague is fated to us," could be stative in isolation, but is dynamic in its context, given the continuation "When we do quicken." On the other hand, "I am abus'd," carries a stative meaning, along the lines of 'I am in an abused state'. Consequently, in the former case, an understood subject, with the A role, is postulated, while in the latter case, there is little or no motivation for an understood agentive subject.

Cajander's (1916) translation of Othello's first soliloquy into Finnish is given in the following, with the case roles of subjects analyzed. The glosses, including the material in brackets, are provided for the convenience of the reader. They are often inelegant and cannot reproduce the rich morphology of Finnish, but may still make it possible to follow the assignment of case roles.

*Oth.*Tuo sepä tavattoman kelpo mies on,	Os
That now extraordinarily good man is,	
Kokenut äly, joka tuntee kaikki	E
Experienced wit, who knows all	
Elämän mutkat. Villiks jos käy haukka,	O
Life's turns. Wild if gets hawk,	
Vaikk' olis sydänsyissäni sen kytkyt,	Os
Although were [in my] heart's fibers its leashes,	
Vihellän pois sen, ilman tuulten valtaan	A
[I] whistle away it, [to the] air's winds' power	
Ja onnens' ohjaan. Sikskö, ett' olen musta	Os

And [to its] fortune's reins. Because[+interrog.] that [I] am black

Enk' osaa mielin kielin laverrella   A
Nor can [I] [with] wit's tongue chatter

Kuin teikarit, tai siks ett' ikä iltaan   A; O
Like dandies, or because that age [to] evening

Jo alkaa painua — ei paljon sentään —   O
Already begins [to] sink — not much though —

Hän mennyt on? ma pettynyt? Nyt inho   A=O; Os; Os
She gone is? I abused? Now loathing

On lohtuni! Oi, avion kirousta,
Is [my] comfort! Oh, marriage's curse,

Ett' olennot nuo vienot ovat meidän,   Os
That creatures those gentle are ours,

Mut niiden sulot ei! Oi, paremp' olla   Os; Os
But their charms not! Oh, better [to] be

Sammakkona ja tyrmän tunkast' elää   O
[A] frog and [on a] dungeon's musty air live

Kuin muiden käytettäväks antaa soppi   A
Than [for] others' use give [a] corner

Rakastetustaan! Se on suurten tuskaa;   Os
[Of one's] beloved! It is great [ones'] pain;

Heill' etuus huonomp' on kuin alhaisolla;   B; B
They have advantage worse than [the] base;

Se välttämätönt' on kuin kuolema;   Os
It inevitable is like death;

Tuo kirous sarvikas jo äidinkohduss'   A
That curse horned already [in] mother's womb

On meille pantu. Tuoss' on hän. Hän viekas?   Os; Os
Is [on] us put. There is she. She cunning?

Oi, silloin taivas itseänsä pilkkaa!   A
Oh, then heaven itself mocks!

Sit' en ma usko.   E
That not I believe.
                    (Cajander (1916, 66))

The case role assignments are undertaken on semantic principles analogous to those in the analysis of the English text. In particular, it is equally possible to view the Agent as designating the typically human perceived willful instigator of action in Finnish as in English (cf. also Siro ([1975] 1977, 32)). Further, a distinction between O and Os, which, as observed above, depends on the division of verbs into dynamic and stative, seems likewise feasible and important in Finnish (cf. Siro ([1975] 1977, 32 f.)).

Regarding case role assignment in Cajander's translation, it may be added that at times his Finnish has a somewhat archaic sound to it, mainly on account of lexical usages and choices that are rare or even obsolete in present-day Finnish. For instance, in the sixth line the import of the word *ohjaan* is perhaps not immediately clear to most speakers of present-day Finnish and the status of the word as a noun, rather than as a verb, becomes clear only on reflection or when a suitable dictionary of Finnish is consulted. However, as a whole, Cajander's Finnish, in spite of the sometimes archaic sounding diction, presents no barrier to understanding and in the overwhelming majority of instances case roles can be assigned with a fair degree of confidence.

Here is the same soliloquy in Jylhä's (1955) translation:

OTHELLO. Rehellinen se mies on ylenmäärin,	Os
Honest that man is abundantly,	
ja mielin kokenein hän oivaltaa	E
And [with a] mind experienced he understands	
kaikk' ihmisvaiheet. Vaimoni jos onkin	Os
all human stages. [My] wife if [she] is [indeed]	
kesyyntymätön haukka, niin, vaikk' ois	Os
untameable hawk, so, even if were	
mun sydänsäikeeni sen jalkahihnat,	
my heart fibers its footstraps,	
vihellän pois sen, myötätuuleen lasken,	A; A
[I] whistle away it, [to a] fair wind [I] release [it],	
niin saalistaa saa ominpäin. Kai siksi,	A
so hunt [it] may [by] itself. Perhaps because	
ett' olen musta, enkä laverrella	Os; A
that [I] am black, nor chatter	
voi niinkuin keikarit, tai siks, ett' iän	A
can [I] like dandies, or because, that [to] age's	
jo iltaan kallistun, — en tosin paljon, —	O
already evening [I] incline — not to be sure much, —	
hän mennyt on, mun pettäen. Vain inho	A=O; A; I
she gone is, me deceiving. Only loathing	
mua lohduttaa. Oi avion kirousta:	
me comforts. Oh marriage's curse:	
olennon omistat noin hemmotellun,	B
creature [you] own so nurtured,	
vaan etpä pyyteitään! Kuin rupikonna	B
but not [her] desires! Like [a] toad	
eläisin tyrmän huuruista ma ennen	O
[would] live [on a] dungeon's vapors I rather	
kuin sopenkaan suon rakkaastani muille.	A
than [even a] corner [I] give [of my] beloved to others.	

Mut se on suurten vitsaus; on heillä　　　　　　Os; B
But it is [the] great [ones'] plague; have they
etuudet huonommat kuin alhaisilla.　　　　　　B
advantages worse than [the] low.
Se osa väistämätön on kuin kuolo;　　　　　　　Os
It [a] part inevitable is like death;
tuo häpeä sarvekas on meille pantu　　　　　　　A
that shame horned is on us put
jo äidin kohdussa. — Kas, Desdemona!
already [in the] mother's womb. — Lo, Desdemona!
Hän viekas? Taivas itseäänkö pilkkais?　　　　　Os; A
She cunning? Heaven itself [would] mock?
Ei, sit' en usko.　　　　　　　　　　　　　　E
No, that [I] not believe.

(Jylhä (1955, 250-1))

Jylhä's translation is of a more recent origin than Cajander's and it has much less of the sometimes archaic sounding diction of Cajander's version. There are very few instances here, if any, where a dictionary needs to be consulted for interpretation prior to case role assignment.

The table below presents a summary of different case roles in the three texts analyzed above.

	Shakespeare	Cajander	Jylhä
A	10	7	10
I			1
E	4	2	2
B	3	2	4
O	4	5	3
Os	14	12	7

The tables below present summaries of different case roles in the other three soliloquies considered and their translations. The assignment of case roles in each case has again followed the principles discussed and illustrated above.

Othello's soliloquy in V.ii:

	Shakespeare	Cajander	Jylhä
A	16	11	13

I	2	2	2
E	5	3	4
B		1	1
O	6	8	9
Os	9	9	7

Iago's soliloquy at II.i. 281 ff.:

	Shakespeare	Cajander	Jylhä
A	15	17	12
I	3	4	4
E	11	10	11
B	1	1	
O	3	2	2
Os	6	5	6

Iago's soliloquy at II.iii.327 ff.:

	Shakespeare	Cajander	Jylhä
A	24	17	21
I	2	1	
E	1	2	1
B	2	3	1
O			1
Os	7	9	6

The findings given here only relate to a subset of Othello's and Iago's soliloquies and the figures must be treated with some caution, pending the outcome of a more comprehensive survey. However, even these findings at the very least establish the point that translations often fail to reproduce the case roles of their originals. Moreover, fluctuations may at times be quite considerable. For instance, the number of Os case roles in Othello's first soliloquy is 14 in the original, but the corresponding figure in Jylhä's translation is considerably lower. Further, the number of A case roles in Othello's soliloquy in V.ii. is 16 in the original but the corresponding figure in Cajander's translation is again much lower. More generally, in the translations considered the widest fluctuations seem to concern these two case roles, whereas fluctuations affecting the I, E, B, and O roles seem smaller, at least as a general tendency. Admittedly, there are fewer of these four types of case roles in the original, but what examples there are of them tend to be in evidence to approximately the same extent in both translations, and the figures tend to be fairly close to the originals. It may be pointed out here that in Iago's soliloquy in II.i. there are quite a large number of E case roles, but much the same figure is found in the two translations.

The A and Os case roles are at the opposite ends of the scale of agentivity set up in Rudanko (1993a, 101 ff.) and therefore they deserve some further attention. (In Rudanko (1993a, 101 ff.) it was argued that from the point of view of agentivity the different case roles considered here line up on the scale of agentivity in the order Agent, Instrument, Experiencer, Benefactive, Object and Object$_{stative}$, with Agents being the most agentive and Objects$_{stative}$ the least so.) As far as the Os case role is concerned, there are some deviations from the original, but they do not seem very systematic in nature. On the other hand, a consideration of the A case role yields more significant results. Apart from one or two exceptions, there seems to be a tendency in this sample for there to be more Agents in Shakespeare's text than in the two translations. This tendency does not appear solely to be a function of the identity of the translator, for both Cajander and Jylhä tend to produce translations that have a smaller number of Agents than the original. The tendency is more marked in Cajander's translations and holds especially of his translations of Othello's soliloquy at III.iii.262 ff. and of Iago's soliloquy at II.iii.327 ff. As far as Jylhä's translations are concerned, the differences in the present sample are smaller and therefore less spectacular, but they still form a consistent pattern of divergence.

Divergences relating to the Agent role are noteworthy because there is also a conceptual content to the notion of agentivity:

> In cognitive terms agentivity amounts to an individual's perception of the world as being molded and shaped by deliberate actions of human beings. In such a world human beings perceive themselves as acting and as "doers." Such perceptions presuppose of course that human beings believe themselves to be capable to undertaking deliberate and willful action and not merely passive patients incapable of action or of seeing the world as shaped by human action. (Rudanko (1993a, 103))

With respect to soliloquies, which are profoundly revealing of a character's innermost thoughts and intentions, it may thus be held that a character using Agents in his or her soliloquies views the world as susceptible to being shaped by purposeful and deliberate human actions. By contrast, a character whose utterances contain only a low number of Agents may be represented as perceiving himself or herself more as a passive victim than as a "doer." The failure of a translation to match the original in respect of agentivity may well entail a shift of artistic and dramatic perspective, at least when the discrepancy is considerable or when it forms a fairly consistent pattern. The discrepancies in the translations of the soliloquies pointed out above arguably give rise to such a shift of dramatic perspective.[1] In these translations the characters in question, Othello and Iago, as the case may be, come to be perceived in a way that diverges from the original in that the language of these characters in their soliloquies, where they disclose their innermost feelings, reveals a conception of the world that is less oriented toward deliberate and purposeful human action than Shakespeare's text implies.

It should be recognized that the translation of Shakespearean drama raises a multiplicity of problems associated with interpretation and the nature of translation equivalence. It is also clear that the selection of four soliloquies out of a full-length tragedy represents a small sample and that very far-reaching conclusions should not be based on it. However, even the present sample demonstrates the need for the translator and the evaluator of translations to be sensitive to distinctions of case roles in translation. This is especially so because divergences affecting for instance the Agent case role may have implications for the interpretation of Shakespeare's classic and of two of its major figures. From a broader perspective, the present article also emphasizes the necessity for exploring, and taking cognizance of, the linguistic foundations of translation, given that thematic roles are articulated and developed in linguistic theory, being anchored in the syntax-semantics interface of linguistic description.

Notes to Chapter 7

1. As argued in Rudanko (1993a, 106 ff.), the Instrument role is at times very close to the Agent role from the point of view of agentivity and it might be suggested that the two case roles should be considered together in the present context. However, the discrepancies between the original and Cajander's and Jylhä's translations of it in respect of agentivity do not change in any significant fashion even if all the Instrument case roles in the speeches were to be considered in conjunction with Agent case roles.

Chapter 8

Interpreting *Othello* in a Popularizing Finnish Production

The purpose of this chapter is to introduce and to discuss a production of Shakespeare's *Othello* in the spring of 1991 that attracted national attention in Finland. The performance in question was staged in the City Theater of Oulu, which is a vibrant University town and sea port of some 100.000 people in Northern Finland, not far from the Arctic Circle.

The production was directed by Hanno Eskola, who kindly made the script used for the production available to the present author; and it is on this script that this inquiry will in the main be based. The focus on the script is not meant to imply that other aspects of the production are unimportant, but it is necessitated by practical considerations and also motivated by the fact that the script represents an objectively existing document of the production that undoubtedly played an important part in guiding the performances of the actors. On the basis of the script, then, comments will be made on two aspects of this twentieth century production. First, it will be shown how this production of the play can clearly be seen as "popularizing," as making Shakespeare more "relevant" to a broader spectrum of theater-goers than those of a cultural highbrow elite. Consideration will then be given to the question of the degree to which the character of the original is lost or preserved, at least in respect of one particular theme. The theme in question is that of agency or agentivity, and it is investigated with reference to a key speech in the play. There is a lively and long-standing tradition of Shakespeare productions in Finland, especially in this century. Normally, such productions are in Finnish, except in the case of touring companies from abroad. There are two "classical" translations into Finnish of some of the most important or often staged plays, including *Othello:* those by Cajander, from the beginning of this century (1916), and by Jylhä, from the middle of the century (1955). However, the production staged in Oulu was based on a text worked out by the director himself.

Eskola's text is not directly comparable with the classical translations, because it is a script for a particular stage production, whereas the translations are standard texts which are subject to revision to suit the needs of various productions. Eskola's text is also more in the nature of an adaptation in a number of ways than are Cajander's and Jylhä's texts. An extract may be helpful to shed light on some aspects of Eskola's script. Here is Iago's speech at I.i.8-39 in response to Roderigo's remark "Thou told'st me, thou didst hold him in thy hate." It will be recalled that the English speech starts "Despise me if I do not: three great ones of the city, / In personal suit to make me his lieutenant, / Oft-capp'd to him, and by the faith of man, / I know my price, I am worth no worse a place" (Ridley ([1958] 1966, 3 f.)).

Jago. ... Mä olisin perverssi jos mä en vihais sitä. Kolme tän kaupungin
It'd be perverse of me if I didn't hate him. Three of the biggest big wigs in town

korstointa kihoo ehdottaa mulle ylennystä Othellon oikeaks kädeks. Mitä
propose me being promoted to Othello's right-hand man. What

tapahtuu? Kihot seisoo räysä kourassa. Kaapii maata. Raapii korvalehtee.
happens? The big shots stand there with their caps in their hands. [They] scratch
the ground with their feet. [They] scratch [their] ear lobes.

Tää ulkomaanpelle paisuttelee itseään. Haluaa vetää omaa linjaa. Mä
This foreign clown swells himself. [He] wants to follow his own course. I've

olen jo tehny valintani. Kukas se on? Mikael Cassio. Tää konttorisolttu
already made my choice. Who is it? Michael Cassio. This office soldier,

tää strateginen luuppisilmä karttalehdellä soittelija etappisika rättimikko
this man with the strategic beady eye, [this] player on a map, [this] pig at the

back, [this] dandy,

kanttiinilotta Mikael Cassio. Kuuluu piireihin. Liepeestä nykijä. Huulella
[this] effeminate kitchen hand Michael Cassio. Belongs to high society. Always
tugging at your sleeve. Hangs

roikkuja. Meinaaja. Meinas päästä naimisiinkin. Jäi meinaamiseks. Miks
on everyone's lips. A man who talks big but gets nothing done. Talked about
getting married, even. Only talk. Why

yks sais hänet kun hän on vielä saamassa monelta.
should one [woman] get him when he is still going to get it from so many.

Even a cursory examination of Eskola's rendering of Iago's speech
reveals some distinctive features of his text. Conspicuously, the speech,
like others in his rendering of the play, is in prose, not in blank verse.
In this respect, the rendering differs from the two "classical" ones, for
the latter follow the original more closely as regards the mode of
speech. At the same time, the choice of the prose medium does not
mean that Eskola's rendering is without its poetic quality. On the
contrary, there are poetic devices employed throughout the text,
including the present passage. For instance, there are examples of
alliteration, as in the second line *korstointa kihoo*, 'the biggest big
wigs'. Further, there are patterns of assonance, as in *Kaapii* and *Raapii*
in the third line, both verbs roughly meaning 'scratch'.

While there is thus a poetic quality to the prose, perhaps the most
outstanding feature of the rendering is the distinctively colloquial
language. As regards the choice of lexical items, the rendering draws
heavily on present-day colloquial Finnish and the associations evoked
by it. Translating such diction into English is almost as difficult as
translating Shakespeare into Finnish in the first place, and the glosses
produced above can hardly do full justice to Eskola's text.
Colloquialisms in this extract include for instance words such as *kihoo*,
'big shots', near the beginning of the extract, and *meinaaja* near the
end. The import of the latter word is hard to convey with one word. It
designates a person who talks a lot about grand plans but is incapable
of putting them into effect.

Not only does the diction of the passage rely on present-day
colloquial Finnish; the grammar does as well. Colloquialisms in the
realm of grammar relate for instance to personal endings. There are
three instances of this in the third line. The verb after the plural noun
phrase *kihot* is inflected for the third person singular, which is a

colloquial feature in Finnish. The subject of the following two verbs is understood to be the same noun phrase, but it has been elided. In these sentences the verb is again inflected for the third person singular, instead of the third person plural. The omission of the subject in the third person in combination with the "wrong" inflection produces a very colloquial effect.

These comments on the diction and grammar of the rendering are partial and only illustrative, but they suffice to establish the colloquial style of the text. Such features of the production may well serve to popularize it, to make it more in tune with the times, and to enable it to reach a wider audience.

We may now turn to the theme of agentivity and the question of how the production under review succeeds in reflecting this aspect of Shakespeare's original play. The notion of agentivity is grounded in linguistic notions of thematic roles and tests of agentivity, as was discussed in chapter 7. The same system of case roles will naturally be applied in this chapter. As far as the selection of textual material is concerned, a soliloquy has again been chosen, for reasons analogous to those in chapter 7. The soliloquy selected is one of the most important in the play, Othello's soliloquy at the beginning of V.ii, the English original of which begins "It is the cause, it is the cause, my soul, / Let me not name it to you, you chaste stars:" (Ridley ([1958] 1966, 177)).

Here is the soliloquy in Eskola's rendering, with case roles of subjects spelled out:

Siks. Jeesus. Just siks. Mä en sano ääneen. Maailma saastuis.	Os; Os;
That's why. Jesus. That's precisely why. But I won't say [it] aloud.	A; O
The world would be contaminated.	

Siks. Ei verta. Ei naarmua hipiään. Pehmeä. Puhdas.	Os; Os;
That's why. No blood. No scratch on the skin. Soft. Clean.	Os; Os;
	Os

Valo valolta pois. Tää liekki ku mä tukahdutan tän tää ei	A; A;
[Switching] one light after another off. This flame	Os
when I extinguish this, this	

ole mitään lopullista. Se syttyy uudestaan ku se sytytetään.	O;
is nothing final. It lights up again when it is lighted.	A/Pass

Jos pimeys kaduttaa. Mikä on tää kuva? Kulunu hyvä.	I; Os;
If darkness makes [one] repent. What is this picture? Used, good.	Os

Elämänliekki. Ku mä sammutan sen mä en tiedä mikä on tää	Os; A;
The fire of life. When I extinguish it, I don't know what is the	E; Os
konsti millä se syttyis taas millä leimauksella uusi kipinä	O; O
means that would bring it back, with what flash	
[would come] a new spark	
ja uusi valo noihin silmiin. Mies poimii ruusun rakkaalleen	A
and a new light into those eyes. A man plucks a rose	
for his loved one	
tää ole rakas mitä rakas mieheltä saa ku mies ojentaa tän	A = O;
this be a dear one, what does the dear one get from a man	B; A
when the man hands over this	
poimitun ruusun? Kuihtumista sellaisen lahjan. Tuoksu jää.	B; O
plucked rose? Withering such a gift. The smell remains.	
Vaikka mut kiskottais taivaaseen ristille roikkumaan	A/Pass;
Even if I were to be dragged to heaven to hang on a cross,	O
tuoksu jää. Yks vielä. Viimeinen. Miks kohtalo on näin kaunis	O; Os
the smell remains. One more thing. The last. Why is destiny	Os; Os
so beautiful	
ku se on niin ruma? Tässä itku auta. Tää menee ny näin.	Os; O;
when it is so ugly? Crying does not help here. This is	O
what happens now.	
Rakkaus rankaisee. Rankaiseminen on rakastamista	I; Os;
Love punishes [one]. Punishment is loving	
miten päin vaan. Mun ei ole pakko mutta mun täytyy.	Os; Os
one way or another. I don't have to but I must.	

Assigning thematic roles to noun phrases in an authentic text is always more difficult but also more rewarding than working with invented examples. As far as the present extract is concerned, one problem concerns sentence fragments, as at the very beginning of the passage. In such fragments, which are often only one word long, it is frequently necessary to supply understood constituents. For instance, in the case of the very first fragment *Siks*, which itself is a colloquial form of *siksi*, 'for that reason', a more fully fleshed out sentence along the lines of 'This is for that reason' may be assumed, and case role assignment proceeds on the basis of the more fully fleshed out sentence.

Another problem area concerns passives. In English passives the notional subject, that is, the subject of the corresponding active sentence, may be expressed in a *by* phrase but may also be omitted. This kind of omission is common in English. In Finnish there is no very idiomatic prepositional construction that would correspond to the English *by* construal, and it is even less common to express the notional subject. On the other hand, even though the notional subject is not expressed, the verb often still retains its dynamic and agentive force. (For the distinction between dynamic and statal passives in English, see Cook (1990, 20 ff.) and Rudanko (1993a, 75-79).) If it does, the corresponding active sentence may be used as a basis for case role assignment.

These comments on case role assignment do not exhaust the problems that may arise when authentic texts are analyzed. (For further discussion of problems in the assignment of case roles, the reader is referred to Rudanko (1993a, 88 f.).) At the same time, it should be emphasized that for the most part, case role assignment can be made with little hesitation, relying on the definitions of the case roles used.

Here is a summary of the incidence of case roles in the soliloquy:

A	9
I	2
E	1
B	2
O	10
Os	19

The explicit analysis of a piece of text enables the investigator to arrive at an index of agentivity. This is simply the percentage of Agents in the text in question. The index of agentivity is helpful in throwing light on the nature of the playwright's fictional world and on the question of how the characters of a play perceive each other and how they perceive themselves. It will be recalled from chapter 7 that agentivity has to do with perceptions of the world in terms of deliberate human action, emanating from free will, whereas lack of agentivity has to do with the absence of free will and of willful action. A high index of agentivity, therefore, privileges the role of free will and of willful human action in the perceptions in question, while a low index indicates a conception where the role of human agency is downplayed.

In the present case the index of agentivity is 21 percent. This may strike one as a relatively low index, since in Shakespeare's original the index of agentivity in this soliloquy is as high as 42 percent (Rudanko (1993a, 104)). However, a consideration of the index of agentivity of a speech in isolation may mean very little, as far as the interpretive significance of the notion is concerned. Broader patterns of agentivity in several speeches or soliloquies in the course of the play should be considered, as was done in Rudanko (1993a). Alternatively, if only one speech can be considered, attention should be focused on changes of agentivity in the course of the speech. This micro-level approach can be applied when the speech in question is of some length, as in the present case.

With regard to Shakespeare's original, it has been observed in the literature, in a nonlinguistic tradition of Shakespeare criticism, how two parts may be discerned in the soliloquy. Wolfgang Clemen describes its beginning as follows:

> Othello enters with unusual self-discipline. He seems to have regained the stately calm and with it the rich poetry which was characteristic of him during the first Acts. We are captivated once again by euphony, whereas in the preceding scenes his language had fallen apart ... (Clemen (1987, 166))

But then there is a change in the soliloquy. Here is Clemen again:

> We note that this soliloquy, like others, does not have one clear line of development leading from beginning to end, but rather a broken inner thread. This emerges most clearly in the last seven lines, which cause us to question in retrospect the firm self-assurance and sovereignty of the opening lines. (Clemen (1987, 170))

In Rudanko (1993a, 104 f.) it was demonstrated how the division of the soliloquy into two parts may be substantiated on the basis of agentivity: in the first part, the index of agentivity is quite high, as high as 55 percent, whereas in the second part it is considerably lower, as low as 25 percent. A case grammar analysis of the speech, then, demonstrates how "the self-assurance and sense of control in the first part of the soliloquy gives way to a perception of the world as outside of human control and dominance in the second part" (Rudanko (1993, 105)).

Taking account of the structuring of Shakespeare's original soliloquy into two parts permits a more sophisticated interpretation of the results of the analysis of Eskola's version produced above. There is no stage direction in Eskola's text that would independently guide us to look for the point of division, but a conceivable place to divide the speech is after the first instance of *tuoksu jää* 'the smell remains'. If this is done, the index of agentivity of the first part is 27 percent, that is, appreciably higher than the overall figure given above, while the figure for the remainder of the speech is only eight percent. The difference can be seen even more clearly in the absolute numbers for the first and second parts of the soliloquy: eight out of thirty case roles are Agents in the first part and only one out of thirteen is an Agent in the second part. By contrast, there are numerous instances of the Os case role in the second part. This is noteworthy because the Os case role is the most antithetical to the Agent role (see Rudanko (1993a, 108-109)).

Overall, then, Eskola's rendering succeeds very well in conveying the shift found with respect to agentivity in the course of the speech in Shakespeare's original text. Indeed, it brings into sharper focus the contrast between the "sense of control" in the first part and the sense of lack of control in the second part.

For practical reasons, the present treatment is limited to the analysis of the one speech. The speech is undoubtedly an important one, but very broad interpretive generalizations should not be based on one speech. Even so, the analysis illustrates the application of the method of case grammar analysis. As far as the results of the analysis are concerned, Eskola's rendering appears at first glance to be rather distant from Shakespeare's original with respect to the index of agentivity. However, at a more nuanced level a case grammar analysis shows how his popularizing script reproduces the shift of perspective in the soliloquy in a way that is very true to the original.

Chapter 9

Not Making a Choice in Dreiser: the Leadup to Hurstwood's Theft in *Sister Carrie*

In his study of *Sister Carrie* Donald Pizer observes that "Dreiser's radical breakthrough in his depiction of man's moral nature occurs ... in his dramatization of the ways in which chance and subconscious desire blend into event. One figure drifts, the other is precipitated into action; but neither makes a choice in the conventional sense of choice" (Pizer (1976, 75)). The purpose of the present article is to investigate the nature of this dramatization. The question is whether it is possible to identify linguistic correlates of a character's making or not making a decision and of his or her drifting, or being precipitated, into a certain action or a certain pattern of behavior. The investigation is focused, by way of a concrete example, on the case of Hurstwood's theft in chapter XXVII of *Sister Carrie* and on how Dreiser depicts the leadup to the theft before the safe shuts itself. This scene speaks directly to the issues of determinism, chance, and free will in Dreiser and the relation of these to each other in Dreiser's first classic. In June Howard's words, "in a sense Hurstwood chooses, but in classically determinist fashion the internal and external forces that shape his actions make nonsense of the notion of free will" (Howard (1985, 44)). The present linguistically oriented investigation, grounded as it is in an objectively verifiable procedure, seeks to elucidate what is going on in the scene and Dreiser's conception of one of his important characters.

The linguistic method to be applied is that of case grammar. The system of case roles is naturally the same as in chapters 7 and 8 and the focus will again be on grammatical subjects. As argued in these earlier chapters, the study of case roles may be viewed as revealing major aspects of the way the author of a piece of communication or of literature conceptualizes the real or the fictional world he or she is presenting. The material to be analyzed in this chapter consists of three paragraphs in chapter XXVII of *Sister Carrie.*

The scene depicted in these paragraphs has been chosen for analysis because it has been taken by critics — including critics not employing a linguistic analysis — to highlight the issues of determinism, chance and free will in Dreiser. Further, no doubt at least in part because of the prominence of these issues in the scene, the episode has been seen to constitute a turning point in Dreiser's classic: the "novel ... pivots on chapter 27, the scene with Hurstwood at the safe of Fitzgerald and Moy's" (Lehan (1969, 63)). In the early part of the novel, Hurstwood, though in conflict with his wife because of his liaison with Carrie, is represented by Dreiser as a man prosperous in his work and confident in his social life. After the scene at the safe of his employers comes his flight, with Carrie, followed by his decline, a slow but inexorable descent into a wretchedness so abject that it would have been unimaginable in the early part of the book.

Here is the analysis of case roles of subjects of sentences in these three paragraphs:

1	The wavering of a mind	Os
2	under such circumstances is an	
3	almost inexplicable thing, and yet	
4	it is absolutely true. Hurstwood	Os; A
5	could not bring himself to act	A
6	definitely. He wanted to think	E; A=E
7	about it—to ponder over it, to	A=E
8	decide whether it were best. He	A=E; Os
9	was drawn by such a keen desire for	I/Pass
10	Carrie, driven by such a state of	I/Pass
11	turmoil in his own affairs that	
12	he thought constantly it would be	E; Os
13	best, and yet he wavered. He did not	O; E
14	know what evil might result	O
15	from it to him—how soon he might	O

16 come to grief. The true ethics	O
17 of the situation never once	
18 occurred to him, and never would	O
19 have, under any circumstances.	
20 After he had all the money in	B
21 the hand bag, a revulsion of feeling	I
22 seized him. He would not do	A
23 it—no! Think of what a scandal	A=E
24 it would make. The police!	Os
25 They would be after him.	A=O
26 He would have to fly, and where?	A=O; A=O
27 Oh, the terror of being a fugitive	Os
28 from justice! He took out the two boxes	A
29 and put all the money back.	A
30 In his excitement he forgot what	E
31 he was doing, and put the sums	A; A
32 in the wrong boxes. As he pushed	A
33 the door to, he thought he remembered	E; E
34 doing it wrong and	A
35 opened the door again. There were	A
36 the two boxes mixed.	Os
37 He took them out and	A
38 straightened the matter, but now	A
39 the terror had gone. Why be afraid?	O; E

(Pizer (1970, 193); line divisions are not Pizer's; lines have been numbered for ease of reference)

It is possible to assign case roles to most grammatical subjects in the extract on the basis of the definitions given in chapter 7 with a fair degree of confidence. Also, in accordance with well-established practice going back to traditional grammar it is assumed that complement clauses dependent on control verbs have their own subjects, as in line 5, where the subject of *act* is understood, in line 6, where the subject of *think* is understood, and in line 7, where the subjects of *ponder* and *decide* are understood. Such subjects, though they lack phonological and lexical realization, are assigned their own case roles. At the same time, there are decisions that are less obvious or less secure. For instance, sometimes there may be felt a degree of uncertainty about assigning coreferential case roles. In this extract coreferential case roles are found with "mental" verbs like *think*, where the roles in question are A and E, represented as A=E, and with verbs of motion like *fly*, where the case roles in question are A and O, represented as A = O. With *fly* in line 26, the assignment seems fairly secure, since the verb expresses motion that is undertaken deliberately. As far as mental verbs like *think* are concerned, their subjects are always Experiencers but they are Agents only where deliberate pondering is involved. It is not always easy to make a judgment on the precise force of a verb of this type, but it would seem that in lines 6 and 7 the "mental" verbs *think, ponder,* and *decide,* which are all complements of *want,* do involve deliberate pondering, as does *think* in line 23, whereas the instances of *think* in lines 12 and 33 do not. As a consequence, the subjects of the former three verbs have been assigned A = E case roles, whereas those of the latter two verbs have been assigned E case roles.

Further, in line 24, the assignment of the Os case role to the subject of *make* may be questioned. It is based on glossing the verb as 'be' or 'constitute' ('Think of what a scandal it would be/constitute'), rather than as 'cause'. (If the latter gloss were adopted, the Os case role would need to be replaced with an I case role.) Also, a sentence fragment such as "and where," in line 26, poses something of a problem, and in this case the analysis above assumes a reconstruction along the lines of 'and where would/should he fly?'.

With respect to another decision on case assignment, it bears noting that the two instances of the I/Pass case role, in lines 9 and 10, are based on the consideration of the corresponding active counterparts of the sentences in question. Underlying this procedure is the division of passives into dynamic and statal or stative, mentioned in chapter 7. It will be recalled that a sentence such as *The door was closed* is ambiguous in isolation. As pointed out, this sentence may have a dynamic interpretation, along the lines of 'someone closed the door', or a statal interpretation, along the lines of 'the door was not open'. The presence of a *by* phrase in a passive is in general an indication of a dynamic passive: thus *The door was closed by John* is not ambiguous, having only the dynamic interpretation. (On the effect of *by* phrases on the interpretation of passives, see Quirk et al. (1985, 170) and Cook (1990, 26).) Where a dynamic interpretation is relevant in a passive, it is appropriate to refer to the corresponding active counterpart of the sentence. The two sentences with the I case roles, in lines 9 and 10, lend themselves to the dynamic interpretation, as is clear when account is taken of the *by* phrases in them.

Finally, it is observed how the second sentence in the extract is negated: "Hurstwood could not bring himself to act definitely." The presence of negation does not affect the assignment of the Agent case roles to the subjects of *bring oneself* and *act*, but it does deny the applicability of these predicates to the subject and therefore deserves to be kept in mind when the results are evaluated.

The case roles having been assigned, it is easy enough to calculate the percentage of Agents in the sample. The number of Agents is 19 and the total number of case roles is 50. This yields an index of agentivity of 38. (As noted in chapter 8, this index is simply the number of Agent case roles as a percentage of the total number of subject case roles.) Admittedly, as regards the question of interpretation, this kind of gross figure means little in isolation, that is, in the absence of more comprehensive work on agentivity in the novel as a whole, other novels by Dreiser, or novels by other authors, or indeed in different types of prose generally.[1] But this does not mean that the type of analysis of one scene as undertaken above is useless or without interest. On the contrary, the micro-level analysis of a scene makes it possible to focus on the question of whether there might be noticeable shifts of agentivity in the course of the scene analyzed. For this purpose, paragraphs suggest themselves, at least tentatively, as units of analysis, since they form natural building blocks that give structure to a text. Naturally, we should be sensitive to the possibility that there may be significant shifts of agentivity within the course of a single paragraph, but it also seems reasonable to look for such shifts from one paragraph to the next. In doing this, some attention may be paid to paragraph size. Very short paragraphs, with only two or three verbs or adjectives assigning case roles, may be important for the development of theme and character and cannot be ignored, but they may not be very suitable by themselves for analyzing shifts in the incidence of case roles. It is probably impossible to put a precise figure on when a paragraph is "long enough" to serve as a unit of analysis for the method applied here, but it would seem that in general a paragraph containing some ten or more verbs or adjectives assigning case roles might reveal certain distinct tendencies in case role assignment and may also permit comparison with adjacent paragraphs, especially when these are of roughly similar size.

Bearing these considerations in mind, we may calculate indices of agentivity with respect to the present sample, in particular for each of the first two paragraphs. The first has 19 verbs or adjectives assigning 22 case roles, and the second has 20 verbs or adjectives assigning 24 case roles.

	para. 1	para. 2
A	5	12
I	2	1
E	6	4
B		1
O	5	3
Os	4	3
index	23 %	50 %

The absolute numbers in these tables are not very large, but when the two paragraphs are compared, the difference between them is quite striking. In the first paragraph the index of agentivity is low, whereas in the second paragraph it is much higher, about double what it is in the first. (It may also be recalled at this point that two of the five Agents in the first paragraph occur in a negated sentence, where the applicability of the agentive predicates to the subject in question is denied.) In the absence of Agents, the first part of the scene is conceptualized mainly in terms of the E, O, and Os case roles. Of these, the Os case role in particular is antithetical to the A case role, as was observed in chapter 7.

In the second paragraph the index of agentivity is much higher. At this point Dreiser represents Hurstwood as regaining his freedom of action and his free will, at least for a moment. A sentence such as *He took out the two boxes and put all the money back* epitomizes the high agentivity of this paragraph, with the verbs *take out* and *put back*. These are prototypically agentive predicates and they easily allow the insertion of the manner adverbial *carefully* and of an *in order to* purpose clause. High agentivity is connected in the paragraph to Hurstwood contemplating not taking the money and in fact putting it back. The high degree of agentivity here may also be important from the point of view of the reader's sympathies, since at the point where Hurstwood seems most in control of his actions, he behaves in a morally more acceptable way.

Going on to the paragraph that immediately follows the extract produced above, it begins "While the money was in his hand the lock clicked. It had sprung!" (Pizer (1970, 193)). In these sentences the three verbs *be*, *click*, and *spring*, are all nonagentive. (The subjects of these three verbs are Os, O, and O, respectively.) An analysis of thematic roles is hardly necessary in order to appreciate that these sentences mean that the safe came to be shut not as the result of a deliberate action on Hurstwood's part but as the result of the operation of chance and of circumstances beyond his control. However, the analysis of thematic relations serves to explain and to reinforce this intuition.

There are aspects of the method of analyzing thematic roles, including the impact of negation, that deserve further attention. More broadly, there is undoubtedly more to the study of free will and determinism than the study of thematic roles. However, since there are linguistic tests of agentivity, the method allows verification and therefore avoids the impressionism that may sometimes adhere in methods of literary analysis. Even in its present form it lends itself to the study of themes such as determinism, chance, and free will in Dreiser, even if only from one particular, linguistic angle. The reader has a sense of the salience of such themes even without studying thematic roles; but the investigation of thematic relations serves to ground intuitive judgments about such themes and their salience in Dreiser's text. In the present study it was shown how the index of agentivity is particularly low in the first paragraph, and the analysis provides an explication of the perception that Hurstwood is not in charge of what is happening at that point. Then there are the shifts of agentivity from one paragraph to the next. They are expressive of the tension between deliberately making a choice, which involves high agentivity, and drifting or being drawn into a choice without being able to choose, or being faced with a fait-accompli, which involves a low degree of, or indeed a total lack of, agentivity. When such shifts are pronounced, as in the present instance, the effect tends correspondingly to heighten or to intensify the tension in the character's mind as perceived by the reader.

The present chapter is confined to the analysis of one episode in *Sister Carrie*. Beyond the concerns of the scene discussed here, there are obvious possibilities of applying the method to other climactic scenes in Dreiser's novels, including, for instance, in *An American Tragedy*. Indeed, this investigation raises the expectation that it ought also to be possible to apply it to scenes in the works of other authors, in order to throw light on the operation of determinism, chance, and free will, from a linguistic point of view, in other fictional worlds.

Notes to Chapter 9

1. In Rudanko (1993a, 101 ff.) it is observed that both in Othello's and in Iago's soliloquies indices of agentivity tended to be higher than 40, but Shakespearean dramatic speech is clearly a different genre and therefore not directly comparable with the present sample.

Chapter 10

Concluding Observations

As observed in the Introduction, the present volume has two general objectives: on the one hand, to shed light on the documentary and literary texts selected for investigation by means of rhetorical and linguistic methods of analysis, and on the other, to see if the application of such theoretical and abstract methods of analysis to concrete data may contribute to the further development of such methods. These two objectives are not independent of each other. On the contrary, in the ideal case progress made toward one objective may lead to progress toward the other and vice versa.

Setting chapter 2 aside, since it is review-like in character and not analytical in the ordinary sense, we may here glance back at the concerns and conclusions of the other chapters. Starting with those dealing with the debate of June 8, 1789, that is, with documentary material, chapter 3 examines the applicability to the debate of Albert Hirschman's theory of the rhetoric of reaction. It is shown that opponents of James Madison's propositions, with James Jackson leading the way, had recourse to an impressive panoply of rhetorical devices intended to thwart Madison's push for change; and that the three theses devised by Hirschman — the perversity thesis, the futility thesis, and the jeopardy thesis — provide a useful framework for the analysis of their reactionary rhetoric. At the same time, it is observed that some additional theses are needed to supplement Hirschman's arsenal. Two of these are procedural, the vicarious rejection thesis — informally, the idea that the proposal for change is not worth debating in the body presently debating it because some other body will reject it anyway — and the vicarious agency thesis — informally, the idea that the proposal for change is not worth debating in the body presently debating it because some other body will make the change anyway. The fact that these two theses are hardly compatible with each other did not prevent both from being put forward in the debate by the anti-amendment side, to block the progress of Madison's propositions. A third thesis, the thesis of timing, is observed to be very common in the debate. It needs to be handled with care and a concern about timing does not always entail an obstructionist attitude. However, taking account of the contexts of the speeches in the debate it is clear that ostensible concerns about timing were indeed used as a mask for opposition to Madison's propositions.

Chapter 4 focuses on rhetorical styles of the main protagonists in the debate from a more narrowly linguistic point of view. It is observed that there are rather striking differences in the rhetorical devices used: Madison, on the pro-amendment side, tends to attend more to the hearers' face wants, whereas Jackson and Vining, key opponents of amendments in the debate, tend not to. The favorite rhetorical figure of the latter two was the rhetorical question. This has generally been considered an off-record strategy, but in the hands of these two Congressmen it was more of an on-record strategy, and a presumptive one at that. One factor contributing to this effect is observed to be the propensity for the orator to answer his own rhetorical questions, to make assurance doubly sure, so to speak. This tendency is especially marked in Congressman Jackson's speeches. No doubt there were other factors besides speaking styles, including Madison's personal stature within the Federalist party, that played a role in the debate and contributed to the outcome, which was a success for Madison, but the question may be asked whether the outcome might not have been in doubt if Madison had likewise adopted a presumptive rhetorical strategy in the debate.

Turning now to the chapters dealing with literary texts, chapter 5 examines the content and the mood of Keats's ode *To Autumn*. It has been suggested in the literature that the ode highlights the themes of absence, death, and desolation. The present treatment accepts the view that plenitude is a dominant trope in the poem, but proceeds to draw on grammatical theory to examine the more precise nature of the use of this trope. Dying is a theme that is present in the poem, but it should be seen in the context of the many activities and processes depicted as taking place. Two patterns of linguistic recurrence, in particular, are examined, and it is argued that the poem displays both a dynamic quality as well as a quality of "never-ceasing." Overall, it is suggested that the mood of the poem is lighter than might be implied by an interpretive emphasis on themes of absence and death and that this less gloomy interpretation is substantiated through the application of a linguistic analysis.

Chapters 6, 7, and 8 deal with aspects of Shakespeare's work, the latter two with its translation. The first employs concepts and hypotheses from conversation analysis to examine two episodes of a confrontational nature between a king (Lear, Leontes) and a person of a lower rank (Kent, Pauline, respectively). The discussion argues that it is helpful to consider the two episodes in combination, because there are so many similarities and parallels between them. It is observed that in both scenes there are "violations" of different types of conversational conventions. Further, such violations do not occur randomly but give substantiation to, and an elucidation of, the impression that a certain measure of audience sympathy accrues to the underdogs in both scenes. The episodes are also examined from the point of view of speech act theory. It is argued that a dominant speech act of the two kings is that of name-calling or dysphemistic epithets. The use of this speech act tends to reinforce the effect of audience sympathy accruing to the underdogs. However, at the end of each episode, Shakespeare restores the rhetorical equilibrium by ensuring that the king regains his composure.

Chapter 7 also deals with data from Shakespeare, but turns to examining Shakespeare in translation. A system of semantically defined case roles is introduced. Such case roles were originally devised for purposes of general linguistic analysis, but the method has been applied to illuminate literary texts. Here it is suggested that it may also be used for cross-linguistic purposes and for the analysis of translations in particular. Key soliloquies in *Othello*, two by Othello and two by Iago, are selected for explicit analysis. Case roles are examined in the original and in two standard or "classic" translations of the soliloquies into Finnish. There is a focus on the Agent case role, for it is argued that the study of agentivity offers an avenue, hitherto largely neglected, for exploring the poet's fictional world and the conception of his characters. This seems especially true of language in a soliloquy, because it is in soliloquies that a Shakespearean character confides his or her innermost thoughts, within the limits of his or her self-knowledge, to the audience. Speech in a soliloquy is also peculiarly revelatory because it is self-initiated, in that a character formulates his speech, in the world of the play, at his or her own discretion, free from the constraints of interactional discourse. In the chapter it is observed that there are differences regarding the extent to which the degree of agentivity of Shakespeare's original text comes across in the two translations.

Chapter 8 takes up a recent production of *Othello* in Finland. The production has been characterized as "popularizing," as designed to open Shakespeare to a broader audience than is often the case today. The linguistic features of what makes the script popularizing are examined. In a second part, a case grammar analysis is given of Othello's famous soliloquy in Act V, to see how case roles in general, and agentivity in particular, are reproduced in this popularizing version of the play. The overall figures of agentivity are lower in the popularizing script than in Shakespeare's original, or in the two standard translations examined in the previous chapter. However, on closer analysis it is observed that the popularizing version succeeds in faithfully representing shifts of agentivity in the course of the speech.

Chapter 9 explores the application of case grammar to one important scene in Theodore Dreiser's *Sister Carrie,* the scene where Hurstwood is at the safe of his employers, poised to commit a crime. The study of case roles is again employed to inquire into the nature of a fictional world. In Dreiser's case, themes relating to the role of determinism and free will in life and in his fiction are important, and it is suggested that the study of case roles may be helpful in providing one angle from which to consider such issues. As in chapter 8, it is emphasized that it is important to be sensitive to shifts of agentivity in the course of a scene. Such shifts are found in the paragraphs examined and their interpretive significance is assessed.

Overall, texts are examined in this book that are either important to, and established as part of, the canon of Western civilization or likely to become so. Such texts have been investigated before from many different points of view, but generally not with the linguistic tools used here. The application of the tools to the present material offers the prospect of investigating other texts of the canon from a fresh angle.

References

Abraham, Henry
    [1967] 1988   *Freedom and the Court. Civil Rights and Liberties in the United States.* Fifth edition. New York: Oxford University Press.

Allan, Keith
    1986   *Linguistic Meaning.* Volume 2. London: Routledge and Kegan Paul.

Allot, Miriam
    1976   *John Keats.* Bradleys, Reading and London: Longman.

Bach, Emmon and Robert Harms, eds.
    1968   *Universals in Linguistic Theory.* New York: Holt, Rinehart and Winston.

Bailey, Charles-James N. and Roger Shuy, eds.
    1973   *New Ways of Analyzing Variation in English.* Washington, D.C.: Georgetown University Press.

Bassnet-McGuire, Susan
    [1980] 1991   *Translation Studies.* Revised edition. London and New York: Routledge.

Bate, Walter Jackson
    1963   *John Keats.* Cambridge: The Belknap Press of Harvard University Press.

Bennison, Neil
    1993   Discourse Analysis, Pragmatics and the Dramatic 'Character': *Tom Stoppard's Professional Foul, Language and Literature* 2: 79-99.

Bolinger, Dwight
    1978   "*Yes-No* Questions Are Not Alternative Questions," in H. Hiz, ed., 87-106.

Bowling Kenneth
1988   "'A Tub to the Whale': the Founding Fathers and the Adoption of the Federal Bill of Rights," *Journal of the Early Republic,* Fall 1988, 223-251.

Bowling, Kenneth
1990   *Politics in the First Congress, 1789-1791.* New York: Garland Publishing.

Brady, Frank, John Palmer, and Martin Price, eds.
1973   *Literary Theory and Structure.* New Haven: Yale University Press.

Brockbank, Philip, ed.
1976   *The Arden Edition of the Works of William Shakespeare Coriolanus.* London: Routledge.

Brown, Penelope and Stephen Levinson
1987   *Politeness: Some Universals in Language Usage.* Cambridge: Cambridge University Press.

Cajander, Paavo
1916   *Shakespearen Draamoja* [Shakespeare's Plays]. *Othello.* Kirjoittanut [written by] William Shakespeare, suomentanut [translated into Finnish by] P. Cajander. Second edition. Helsinki: Suomalaisen Kirjallisuuden Kirjapaino Oy.

Chomsky, Noam
1986   *Barriers.* Cambridge, Mass.: The MIT Press.

Clemen, Wolfgang
1987   *Shakespeare's Soliloquies.* London: Methuen.

Cole, Peter and Jerry Morgan, eds.
1975   *Syntax and Semantics,* volume 3, *Speech Acts.* New York: Academic Press.

Cook, Walter
1979   *Case Grammar: Development of the Matrix Model (1979-1978).* Washington, D.C.: Georgetown University Press.

Cook, Walter
1989   *Case Grammar Theory.* Washington, D.C.: Georgetown University Press.

Cook, Walter
1990   "Passive Semantics: Ambiguity of the Short Passive," *The Georgetown Journal of Languages & Linguistics* 1, 25-30.

Cornford, F. M.
[1908] 1953   *Microcosmographia Academica. Being a Guide for the Young Academic Politician.* Fifth edition. Cambridge: Bowes and Bowes.

Coulthard, Malcolm
1977   *An Introduction to Discourse Analysis.* London: Longman.

Covelli, Lucille and Stephen Murray
1980   "Accomplishing Topic Change," *Anthropological Linguistics* 22: 382-389.

Davenport, Arnold
1959   "A Note on 'To Autumn'," in Kenneth Muir, ed., 95-101.

Dijk, Teun van
1981   *Studies in the Pragmatics of Discourse.* The Hague: Mouton.

Downes, William
1989   "Discourse and Drama: King Lear's 'Question' to his Daughters," in W. van Peer, ed., 225-257.

Dubrow, Heather
1987   *Captive Victors: Shakespeare's Dramatic Poems and Sonnets.* Ithaca: Cornell University Press.

Dumbauld, E.
1957   *The Bill of Rights and What It Means Today.* Norman, Oklahoma: University of Oklahoma Press.

Ellis-Fermor, Una
1946   *The Frontiers of Drama.* New York: Oxford University Press.

Eskola, Hanno
MS   *William Shakespeare: Othello.* Suomentanut [translated into Finnish by] Hanno Eskola.

Fillmore, Charles
1968   "The Case for Case," in Emmon Bach and Robert Harms, eds., 1-88.

Finney, Claude
[1936] 1963   *The Evolution of Keats's Poetry.* New York: Russell and Russell.

Freeman, Donald
1978   "Keats's 'To Autumn': Poetry as Process and Pattern," *Language and Style* 11, 3-17.

Gales, Joseph
1834   *The Debates and Proceedings in the Congress of the*
               United States. With an Appendix containing Important
               State Papers and Public Documents and all the Laws
               of a Public Nature. Volume I, Comprising (with
               volume II) the period from March 3, 1789 to March
               3, 1791, inclusive. Compiled from authentic materials
               by Joseph Gales, Senior. Washington: Gales and
               Seaton.
Gittings, Robert
1970   *Letters of John Keats. A New Selection.* London:
               Oxford University Press.
Greenbaum, Sidney, Geoffrey Leech, and Jan Svartvik, eds.
1980   *Studies in English Linguistics for Randolph Quirk.*
               London: Longman.
Gruber, Jeffrey
1967   "*Look* and *See*," *Language* 43, 937-947.
Gruber, Jeffrey
1976   *Lexical Structures in Syntax and Semantics.*
               Amsterdam: North-Holland Publishing Company.
Gwynn, Frederick
1952   "Keats, Autumn, and Ruth," *Notes and Queries* 197,
               471-472.
Halliday, M. A. K. and Ruqaiya Hasan
1976   *Cohesion in English.* London: Longman.
Hartman, Geoffrey H.
1973   "Poem and Ideology: A Study of Keats's 'To
               Autumn'," in Frank Brady et al., eds., 305-330.
Herman, Vimala
1991   "Dramatic Dialogue and the Systematics of Turn-
               Taking," *Semiotica* 83: 97-121.
Hirschman, Albert
1991   *The Rhetoric of Reaction. Perversity, Futility,*
               Jeopardy. Cambridge, Mass. and London, England:
               The Belknap Press of Harvard University Press.
Hiz, H. ed.
1978   *Questions.* Dordrecht: D. Reidel.
Howard, June
1985   *Form and History in American Literary Naturalism.*
               Chapel Hill, N.C.: The University of North Carolina

Press.

Hudson, Richard
1975   "The Meaning of Questions," *Language* 51, 1-31.
Jack, Ian
1967   *Keats and the Mirror of Art.* Oxford: Clarendon
            Press.
Jackendoff, Ray
1972   *Semantic Interpretation in Generative Grammar.*
            Cambridge, Mass.: The MIT Press.
Jugurtha, Lillie
1985   *Keats and Nature.* New York: Peter Lang.
Jylhä, Yrjö
1955   *William Shakespearen Suuret Draamat II* [William
            Shakespeare's Great Plays II]. *Hamlet, Othello.*
            Suomentanut [translated into Finnish by] Yrjö Jylhä.
            Helsinki: Otava.
Ketcham, Ralph
[1971] 1990 *James Madison. A Biography.* Charlottesville:
            University Press of Virginia.
Kiparsky, Paul
1973   "The Role of Linguistics in a Theory of Poetry,"
            Daedalus 102, 231-244.
Labov, William and David Fanshel
1977   *Therapeutic Discourse: Psychotherapy and
            Conversation.* Orlando: Academic Press.
Lakoff, George
1966   "Stative Adjectives and Verbs," *National Science
            Foundation 17.* Cambridge, Mass.: Computational
            Laboratory, Harvard University.
Leavis, F. R.
[1936] 1949 *Revaluation.* London: Chatto and Windus.
Lehan, Richard
1969   *Theodore Dreiser. His World and his Novels.*
            Carbondale and Edwardsville: Southern Illinois
            University Press.
Levin, Bernard
1991   "Even about the Dead They Lie," *The Times* (August
            1), 14.
Levinson, Stephen
1983   *Pragmatics.* Cambridge: Cambridge University Press.

Macksey, Richard
1984   "'To Autumn' and the Music of Mortality," in Arden Reed, ed., 263-308.
Mayhead, Robin
1967   *John Keats.* Cambridge: Cambridge University Press.
McElroy, John H.
1989   *Finding Freedom: America's Distinctive Cultural Formation.* Carbondale and Edwardsville: Southern Illinois University Press.
Muir, Kenneth, ed.
1959   *John Keats. A Reassessment.* Liverpool University Press.
Muir, Kenneth, ed.
[1952] 1972   *The Arden Edition of the Works of William Shakespeare King Lear.* London: Methuen.
Murry, John M.
[1925] 1964   *Keats and Shakespeare. A Study of Keats' Poetic Life from 1816 to 1820.* London: Oxford University Press.
Music, Bradley, Randolph Graczyk, and Caroline Wiltshire
1989   *CLS 25. Papers from the 25th Annual Regional Meeting of the Chicago Linguistic Society. Part Two: Parasession on Language in Context.* Chicago: Chicago Linguistic Society.
OED
1971   *The Compact Edition of the Oxford English Dictionary.* Oxford: Oxford University Press.
Orasanu, Judith, Mariam Slater, and Leonore Loeb, eds.
1979   *Language, Sex and Gender.* Annals of The New York Academy of Sciences 327. New York: The New York Academy of Sciences.
Pafford, J. H. P., ed.
[1963] 1968   *The Arden Edition of the Works of William Shakespeare The Winter's Tale.* London: Methuen.
Peer, Willie van, ed.
1989   *The Taming of the Text: Explorations on Language, Literature and Culture.* London: Routledge.
Pizer, Donald, ed.
1970   *Sister Carrie. An Authoritative Text.* Background and Sources. Criticism. New York: W. W. Norton.

Pizer, Donald
1976   *The Novels of Theodore Dreiser. A Critical Study.*
              Minneapolis, Minn.: University of Minnesota Press.

Pope, Emily
1976   *Questions and Answers in English.* The Hague:
              Mouton.

Quirk, Randolph, Sidney Greenbaum, Geoffrey Leech and Jan Svartvik
1985   *A Comprehensive Grammar of the English Language.*
              London: Longman.

Reed, Arden, ed.
1984   *Romanticism and Language.* Ithaca: Cornell
              University Press.

Ricks, Christopher
[1974] 1984   *Keats and Embarrassment.* Oxford: Clarendon Press.

Ridley, M. R.
1933   *Keats' Craftsmanship.* Oxford: Clarendon Press.

Ridley, M. R., ed.
[1958] 1966   *The Arden Edition of the Works of William
              Shakespeare Othello.* London: Methuen.

Rudanko, Juhani
1989   *Complementation and Case Grammar. A Syntactic
              and Semantic Study of Selected Patterns of
              Complementation in Present-Day English.* Albany,
              N.Y.: State University of New York Press.

Rudanko, Juhani
1993a   *Pragmatic Approaches to Shakespeare: Essays on
              OTHELLO, CORIOLANUS and TIMON OF ATHENS.*
              Lanham, Maryland and London: University Press of
              America.

Rudanko, Juhani
1993b   "On Some Aspects of Rhetorical Questions in
              English," *Studia Neophilologica* 65, 29-36.

Rutland, Robert
1983   *The Birth of the Bill of Rights, 1776-1791.* Boston:
              Northeastern University Press.

Sacks, Harvey, Emanuel Schegloff and Gail Jefferson
1974   "A Simplest Systematics for the Organization of
              Turn-Taking for Conversation," *Language* 50: 696-
              735.

Sag, Ivan
1973   "On the State of Progress on Progressives and
               Statives," in Charles-James N. Bailey and Roger
               Shuy, eds., 83-95.
Schiffrin, Deborah
1987   *Discourse Markers.* Cambridge: Cambridge
               University Press.
Searle, John
1969   *Speech Acts: an Essay in the Philosophy of Language.*
               Cambridge: Cambridge University Press.
Searle, John
1975   "Indirect Speech Acts," in P. Cole and J. Morgan,
               eds., 59-82.
Siro, Paavo
[1975] 1977   *Sijakielioppi.* Second, revised edition. Helsinki: Oy
               Gaudeamus Oy.
Stillinger, Jack
1974   *The Texts of Keats's Poems.* Cambridge, Mass.:
               Harvard University Press.
Stillinger, Jack, ed.
1978   *The Poems of John Keats.* Cambridge, Mass.: The
               Belknap Press of Harvard University Press.
Svartvik, Jan
1980   "*Well* in Conversation," in Sidney Greenbaum,
               Geoffrey Leech, and Jan Svartvik, eds., 167-178.
Swaminathan, S. R.
1981   *The Still Image in Keats's Poetry.* Salzburg Studies in
               English Literature under the Direction of Professor
               Erwin A. Stuerzl, 98. Universitaet Salzburg: Institut
               fuer Anglistik und Amerikanistik.
Tannen, Deborah
1989   "Interpreting Interruption in Conversation," in
               Bradley Music, et al., eds., 266-287.
Thorne, Barrie, Cheris Kramarae, and Nancy Henley, eds.
1983   *Language, Gender and Society.* Rowley, Mass.:
               Newbury House.
Veit, Helen, Kenneth Bowling, and Charlene Bickford, eds.
1991   *Creating the Bill of Rights.* Baltimore and London:
               The Johns Hopkins University Press.

Vendler, Helen
1983   *The Odes of John Keats.* Cambridge, Mass.: The Belknap Press of Harvard University Press.

Ward, Aileen
1963   *John Keats. The Making of a Poet.* London: Secker and Warburg.

West, Candace
1978   *Communicating Gender: A Study in Dominance and Control in Conversation.* Santa Barbara: University of California Doctoral Dissertation.

West, Candace
1979   "Against Our Will: Male Interruptions of Females in Cross-Sex Conversation," in Judith Orasanu et al., eds., 81-97.

West, Candace and Don Zimmerman
1983   "Small Insults: a Study of Interruptions in Cross-Sex Conversations between Unacquainted Persons," in Barrie Thorne et al., eds., 102-117.

Index

Abraham, Henry, 8
agentivity, 92, 93, 99-101, 104, 106, 108-110, 115, 117, 118
Allan, Keith, 41, 42, 77
Allot, Miriam, 60
amendments, first, 8; structural, 9, 25; procedural, 9, 25
American Herald and the Worcester Recorder, The, 14
Ames, Fischer, 44

Bassnet-McGuire, Susan, 89
Bate, Walter Jackson, 64, 67
Bennison, Neil, 85n.4
Bill of Rights, American, 1, 4, 7-10, 17, 20-23, 26, 32, 47, 55, 56; British, 7
Bolinger, Dwight, 37
Boudinot, Elias, 13, 15
Bowling, Kenneth, 9-11, 14, 15, 56
Brockbank, Philip, 86, 88
Brown, Penelope and Stephen Levinson, 42, 43, 45, 46, 48n.2, 81; apology, 45; question, hedge, 45; quality

hedge, 46
Burke, Aedanus, 12, 27, 28

Cajander, Paavo, 89, 94-99, 101, 104
case roles, Agent, 90-93, 96, 99-101; Instrument, 90, 99, 101; Experiencer, 91, 99; Object, 91, 95, 99; Object$_S$, 91, 95, 98, 99
Chomsky, Noam, 90
Clemen, Wolfgang, 109
Constitutional Convention, 9, 10
Cook, Walter, 91, 94, 108, 114
Cornford, F. M., 33n.1; "the Time is not Ripe" thesis, 33n.1; reference to the thesis of timing, 33n.1
Coulthard, Malcolm, 85n.4
Covelli, Lucille and Stephen Murray, 85n.5

Davenport, Arnold, 62, 64, 68n.2
Dijk, Teun van, 77
Downes, William, 85n.3, 85n.4

Dreiser, Theodore, 4; *An American Tragedy,* 117; *Sister Carrie* 4, 111-117, 122
Dubrow, Heather, 86n.9
Dumbauld, E., 9
dynamic and stative verbs, 65, 66. See *also* passive sentences.
dysphemistic epithets, analysis of, 82-84

Ellis-Fermor, Una, 90
Eskola, Hanno, 103-106, 110

face, 48n.2; positive, 48n.2; negative, 42, 43, 48n.2
Fillmore, Charles, 90, 91
Finney, Claude, 68n.4
Foster, William, 34, 45
Freeman, Donald, 61

Gales, Joseph, 7, 11-17, 21-31, 36, 44, 49-57
Gazette of the United States, The, 13-15
Gerry, Elbridge, 9, 12-14, 16, 56
Gittings, Robert, 63, 68n.4
Goodhue, Benjamin, 11, 28, 31
Gruber, Jeffrey, 91, 92
Gurney, Ian, 85n.8
Gwynn, Frederick, 68n.2

Halliday, M. A. K. and Ruquaiya Hasan, 77
Hartman, Geoffrey H., 65
Herman, Vimala, 85n.4, 85n.6
Herald of Freedom and the

Federal Advertiser, The, 14
Hirschman, Albert, 2, 19, 20, 27, 30-32, 33n.1, 119; futility thesis, 19, 20, 22-24, 26; imminent danger thesis, 30; jeopardy thesis, 19, 20, 27, 30; perversity thesis, 19, 21
Howard, June, 111
Hudson, Richard, 36, 39
Hurford, James, 85n.1

imperative construction, 66
interruptions, supportive, 79; disruptive, 79, 80, 83

Jack, Ian, 62, 68n.2
Jackendoff, Ray, 91
Jackson, James, 3, 11, 12, 16, 17, 21-23, 26-29, 31, 32, 35-40, 42-50, 55, 119, 120
Jefferson, Thomas, 10
Jugurtha, Lillie, 63, 64
Jylhä, Yrjö, 89, 96-99, 101, 104

Keats, John, *Ode to a Nightingale,* 64; *On a Grecian Urn,* 63; *To Autumn,* 3, 59-69, 120
Ketcham, Ralph, 46
Kiparsky, Paul, 61

Labov, William and David Fanshel, 78
Lakoff, George, 65, 66, 68n.5
Laurance (Lawrence, Lawrance), John, 13, 15-17
Leavis, F. R., 60
Lee, R. B., 13-15

Lehan, Richard, 112
Lehrer, Adrienne, 68n.1
Levin, Bernard, 6, 8
Levinson, Stephen, 77, 85n.5
Livermore, Samuel, 13, 14, 16, 24

Macksey, Richard, 65, 67-69n.6
Madison, James, 1-3, 7, 10-17, 20-32, 35-36, 46-49, 52-57, 119, 120
Mason, James, 9
Mayhead, Peter, 64
McElroy, John H., 5, 6, 8
McNiece, Gerald, 68n.1
Monroe, James, 10
Muir, Kenneth, 73
Murry, John Middleton, 60, 63

obligations honored thesis, 31
OED, 62, 65

Pafford, J. H. P., 75
Page, John, 12, 13, 15, 29, 30, 56
passive sentences, dynamic, 94, 108, 114; statal (stative), 94, 108, 114
Pizer, Donald, 111, 116
politeness, negative, 46; strategies of, 45, 46
Pope, Emily, 37-39
Providence Gazette and Country Journal, The, 14

Quirk, Randolph et al., 37, 66, 114

Reynolds, J. R., Keats's letter

to, 60, 63-65
Ricks, Christopher, 60, 65
Ridley, M. R., 67, 77, 92-93, 104, 106
Royle, Nicholas, 64, 65, 68n.1
Rudanko, Juhani, 3, 37, 77, 82, 85n.4, 85n.8, 90, 92-94, 99, 101n.1, 108, 109, 118n.1
Rutland, Robert, 5, 9-11, 22, 36, 56, 57

Sacks, Harvey et al., 76, 77, 79
Sag, Ivan, 68n.5
Schiffrin, Deborah, 78
Searle, John, 40, 41, 48n.1; view of speech acts, 80, 81; analysis of requesting, 80, 81, 85n.7; view of questions as indirect directives, 81
Sedgwick, Thomas, 55, 56
Shakespeare, William, *Coriolanus,* 86-88; *King Lear,* 3, 71-73, 78-85, 121; *Othello,* 3, 77, 78, 92, 93, 103-110, 121, 122; *The Winter's Tale,* 3, 71, 73-75, 78, 79, 81-85, 121;
Shakespearean soliloquies, 90, 106, 108-110, 121
Sherman, Roger, 9, 12-14, 17, 22-24, 55, 59
Siro, Paavo, 95
Smith, William (of South Carolina), 11-13, 30, 31
Stillinger, Jack, 67, 68n.1, 68n.4
Sumter, Thomas, 13, 14
Svartvik, Jan, 78

Swaminathan, S. R., 61, 68n.2

Tannen, Deborah, 79
thematic roles (relations). *See* case roles.
thesis, obligations honored, 31; of timing, 27-30, *see also* Cornford, F. M.; vicarious agency, 26, 32; vicarious rejection, 24-26, 32. *See also* Hirschman, Albert.
topic development, 77, 78

Veit, Helen, Kenneth Bowling and Charlene Bickford, eds., 14
Vendler, Helen, 61-65
vicarious agency thesis, 26, 32
vicarious rejection thesis, 24-26, 32
Vining, John, 3, 12-14, 16, 25, 26, 35, 36, 38-40, 43-52, 55, 56, 120

Ward, Aileen, 60
West, Candace, 79
West, Candace and Don Zimmerman, 79
White, Alexander, 12
Woodhouse, Richard, Keats's letter to, 68n.4